COMPLETE
ScienceSmart®

Grade 7

Table of Contents

Section 1

Understanding Life Systems

Students will study ecosystems and their biotic and abiotic elements. They will understand how energy is transferred through producers, consumers, and decomposers within an ecosystem. Furthermore, students will learn that matter is cycled in various cycles in the environment. They will also learn that successions, including primary and secondary successions, occur naturally over time. The impacts of human activities on ecosystems and measures taken by the government to protect ecosystems will also be discussed.

Unit 1	Ecosystems	8
Unit 2	Transfer of Energy in Ecosystems	14
Unit 3	Cycles in the Environment	20
	Experiment	26
Unit 4	Stability and Change in Ecosystems	28
Unit 5	Human Activities and Ecosystems	34
Unit 6	Controlling Human Impacts	40
	Experiment	46
	Review	48
	Scientists at Work	54
	Cool Science Facts	55

Understanding Structures and Mechanisms

Students will classify structures as frame, shell, and solid structures, as well as combinations of them. They will investigate the centre of gravity and symmetry of a structure and how they affect a structure's stability. The factors that affect the amount of force acting on a structure will also be studied. Students will explore what can cause structures to fail and what factors should be considered to prevent structural failures. Moreover, they will examine the properties of different materials and how these properties make the materials suitable for certain structures.

Unit 1	Basic Structures	60
Unit 2	Centre of Gravity	66
Unit 3	Forces and Structures	72
	Experiment	78
Unit 4	More about Structures	80
Unit 5	Loads and Structural Failure	86
Unit 6	Materials and Structures	92
	Experiment	98
	Review	100
	Scientists at Work	106
	Cool Science Facts	107

Table of Contents

Understanding Matter and Energy

Students will be introduced to the particle theory of matter and understand that all matter is made up of particles. They will explore the distinction among pure substances, mechanical mixtures, and solutions using the theory. Students will learn to identify the solute and solvent in a solution and explore the common processes used to separate mixtures. Additionally, students will learn how to dispose of harmful substances and use non-toxic substances in place of toxic ones.

Unit 1	The Particle Theory of Matter	112
Unit 2	Pure Substances and Mixtures	116
Unit 3	Solutions and Mechanical Mixtures	120
	Experiment	124
Unit 4	Solutions	126
Unit 5	Separating Mixtures	130
Unit 6	Substances and the Environment	134
	Experiment	138
	Review	140
	Scientists at Work	146
	Cool Science Facts	147

Understanding Earth and Space Systems

Students will examine the renewable and non-renewable sources of heat. They will investigate the effects of heat on different states of matter and how the particle theory of matter explains these effects. Students will also be introduced to the three ways of heat transfer: conduction, convection, and radiation. They will learn that some materials conduct heat well while others insulate people and things from heat, and some materials absorb heat while others reflect heat. Moreover, they will examine the greenhouse effect through their understanding of heat.

Unit 1	Sources of Heat	152
Unit 2	Heat and the Particle Theory of Matter	156
Unit 3	Heat Transfer: Conduction	160
	Experiment	164
Unit 4	Heat Transfer: Convection	166
Unit 5	Heat Transfer: Radiation	170
Unit 6	The Greenhouse Effect	174
	Experiment	178
	Review	180
	Scientists at Work	186
	Cool Science Facts	187
	Answers	191
	Trivia Questions	207

Dear Parents and Guardians,

Learning science begins with curiosity! Complete ScienceSmart is an innovative curriculum-based workbook series which guides your young explorer through a variety of level-appropriate activities to help him or her master and relate the basic concepts of science and technology, which in turn, fulfills his or her curiosity in understanding both the natural and human-made worlds.

Designed and targeted for children from Grades 1 to 8, this resourceful workbook comprises four strands: Life Systems, Structures and Mechanisms, Matter and Energy, and Earth and Space Systems. Each strand contains six correlated units, two hands-on experiments, and one review. Each unit helps your child investigate a new concept and stimulates his or her interest in learning through scientific vocabulary, informative examples and passages, real-world applications, fun and relevant illustrations, and easy-to-follow activities. Reviews are provided at the end of the units to help your child consolidate his or her understanding of the topics. Also included is a concise answer key, which allows you to provide feedback and evaluate your child's progress.

Developing an inquisitive mind is essential in learning. Through our thoughtfully designed hands-on experiments, your child will be encouraged to ask questions, make observations, think critically, and explain his or her reasoning. Most importantly, your child will discover that learning science is all about trial and error.

Furthermore, "Scientists at Work", "Cool Science Facts", "Trivia Questions", and our bonus online resources are provided to inspire and motivate your young scientist through his or her journey of discovering this world!

Complete ScienceSmart is a series of workbooks that helps foster your child's curiosity and develop the skills needed for his or her future scientific inquiry.

Your Partner in Education,
Popular Book Company (Canada) Limited

Section 1

Understanding Life Systems

Scan this QR code or go to Download Centre at **www.popularbook.ca** for some fun scientific explorations!

EXPLORATION

1 **Cleaning Up Oil Spills**
Explore different methods to clean up oil spills.

EXPLORATION

2 **An Ecosystem in a Bottle**
Investigate the relationships between the elements in an ecosystem.

1 Ecosystems

Living things depend on living and non-living things to survive. An ecosystem is where this survival happens. It can be part of a greater ecosystem, contain smaller ecosystems, and overlap with other ecosystems. In this unit, you will examine the parts that make up an ecosystem.

After completing this unit, you will

- know what an ecosystem is.
- know what biotic and abiotic elements of an ecosystem are.
- understand that biotic and abiotic elements of an ecosystem interact with themselves and each other.

Hi, giraffe. Do you want to come home with me?

No, thank you. This savannah provides me with what I need. It's the perfect place for me.

Vocabulary

ecosystem: a system of interactions between organisms and their environment

abiotic: not living

biotic: living or once-living

organism: a single life form, like a plant or an animal

photosynthesis: the process of turning sunlight into food

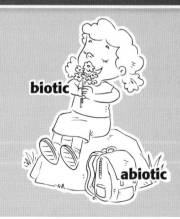

biotic

abiotic

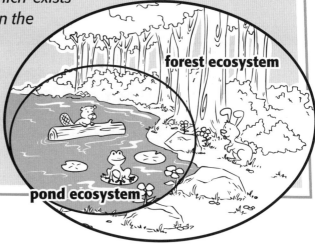

Extension

Ecosystems exist within larger ecosystems. If there is a forested area near your house, you can easily see this. A fallen log is an ecosystem that may exist within a pond or marsh ecosystem, which exists in a forest ecosystem, which exists within the ecosystem of Earth.

Examine other natural areas around you to see if you can spot ecosystems that exist within larger ecosystems.

forest ecosystem

pond ecosystem

A. Fill in the blanks with the given words. Then circle the correct words to identify and describe the ecosystem in the picture.

An 1._____ is a system where 2._____ and non-living things interact. An ecosystem's living members make up a 3._____ , and the ecosystem is their 4._____ , providing them with what they need to live. Many different species of 5._____ form an ecosystem, but their 6._____ can vary, depending on their roles.

> community
> living
> populations
> habitat
> ecosystem
> organisms

7. **desert / temperate / rainforest** ecosystem

   temperature: **cold / warm**

   humidity: **wet / dry**

   species variety: **small / large**

B. **Use the picture clues to name each ecosystem and sort the biotic and abiotic elements of each one. Then write one more example for each.**

coyote	salt water	sage	octopus
rock	owl	sun	cactus	sand
kelp	fresh water	rattlesnake	air
dolphin	algae	gull	

The abiotic elements may overlap.

1.

_____ ecosystem

Biotic Elements

_____

_____

_____

_____

_____

e.g. _____

Abiotic Elements

_____

_____

_____

_____

_____

e.g. _____

2.

_____ ecosystem

Biotic Elements

_____

_____

_____

_____

_____

e.g. _____

Abiotic Elements

_____

_____

_____

_____

_____

e.g. _____

C. For each scenario, put circles or squares around each pair of ecosystem elements. Then identify the type of interaction the elements have.

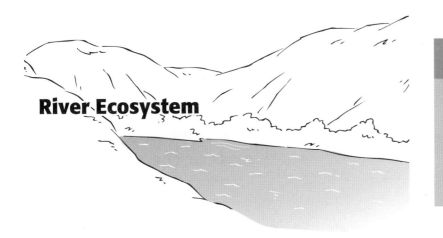

River Ecosystem

Types of Interactions

- biotic/biotic
- biotic/abiotic
- abiotic/abiotic

1. Small (mud) particles move with the stream and are deposited in places where the (water) slows.

2. Mussels burrow under the stream bed to avoid being moved along with the current.

3. Young fish eat insect larvae, which are the offspring of insects that feed on the remains of adult fish.

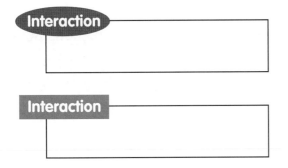

4. If disturbed, sediment makes the water murky. This blocks the sunlight that marine plants need to make food.

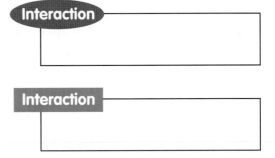

D.   Read the passage. Then answer the questions.

An Amazing Interaction:
Photosynthesis

One of the most interesting interactions between biotic and abiotic elements in any ecosystem happens between green plants and the sun, water, and air.

Green plants use their leaves and other green parts to make their own food, a sugar, through a process called photosynthesis. Inside all green plants are tiny parts called chloroplasts where photosynthesis takes place. Within each chloroplast is a chemical called chlorophyll that is essential to photosynthesis and makes plants appear green. Chlorophyll, along with the carbon dioxide that plants take in, and the water that they absorb using their roots, react with sunlight to make sugar. The process of photosynthesis also produces oxygen as waste. Hence, plants (biotic elements in an ecosystem) interact with sunlight, water, and carbon dioxide (abiotic elements in an ecosystem) to make sugar and oxygen (abiotic elements) in a fascinating and essential interaction.

Photosynthesis makes many other essential interactions possible: animals breathe in this waste oxygen, and animals eat plants or eat other animals that have eaten plants. In fact, most life is possible because of photosynthesis.

1. Write the terms that match the descriptions.

   a. a chemical that makes a plant green   _____

   b. the process by which a green plant makes food   _____

   c. a waste gas produced during photosynthesis   _____

   d. parts of a plant that contain chlorophyll   _____

   e. food that a green plant makes   _____

2. Colour the leaf and label the elements involved in photosynthesis.

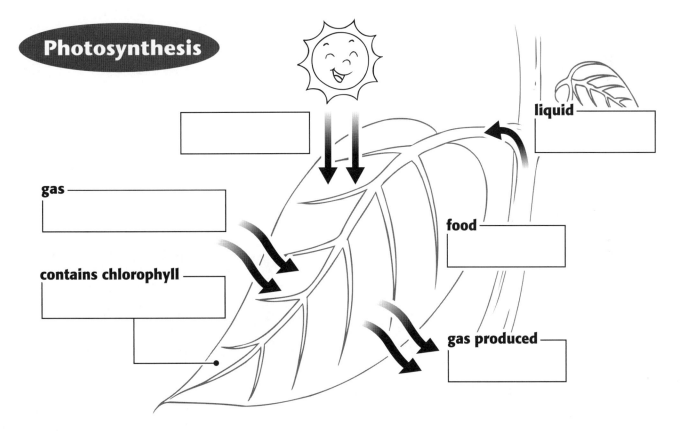

3. Write an example of each type of interaction that is mentioned in the passage.

   biotic/biotic   biotic/abiotic   abiotic/abiotic

   _____   _____   _____

2 Transfer of Energy in Ecosystems

A producer uses sunlight to make food, and this food provides the producer with the energy it needs to live, grow, and reproduce. Some of the producer's energy is transferred to a consumer once the producer is eaten. In this unit, you will examine how energy is transferred from one organism to another in an ecosystem.

After completing this unit, you will

- understand how energy is transferred in an ecosystem.

- understand the roles of producers, consumers, and decomposers within an ecosystem and the interactions among them.

Shhhh. Don't make so much noise. That black bear is an omnivore. It might want to eat us if it notices us.

Vocabulary

carnivore: eats only animals

herbivore: eats only plants

omnivore: eats both plants and animals

bacteria: single-celled organisms that live everywhere on Earth

fungi: organisms that recycle nutrients by decomposing other organisms

carnivore

Bacteria are tiny organisms that are everywhere. You cannot get away from them, and you would not want to! There are many times more bacteria in our bodies than there are human body cells. Few of them are harmful, and some have no effect at all. In fact, many are necessary for our survival: among other things, they help us digest food, break down nutrients, and fight off bad bacteria.

streptococcus pyogenes
causes strep throat

bacteroides
helps us digest food

A. Fill in the blanks with the given words. Then complete the diagram with the words in bold.

| waste | fungi | food | herbivores | growth | carnivores | nutrients |

Plants convert energy from the sun into 1._____ . They are **producers**. 2._____ and omnivores eat plants to get energy. They are **primary consumers**. 3._____ and omnivores eat primary consumers. They are **secondary consumers**.

Decomposers, such as bacteria and 4._____ , convert plants and animals and their 5._____ into carbon dioxide and 6._____ . Nutrients become part of the soil and are essential to plant 7._____ .

8.

9.

The Food Cycle

10.

11.

B. **Name each part of the food cycle. Sort each organism into the correct box. Then answer the questions.**

decomposers
producers
secondary consumers
primary consumers

human   mushroom   deer
cow   wolf   millipede
apple tree   mole   grass   squirrel

1. The **Food Cycle**

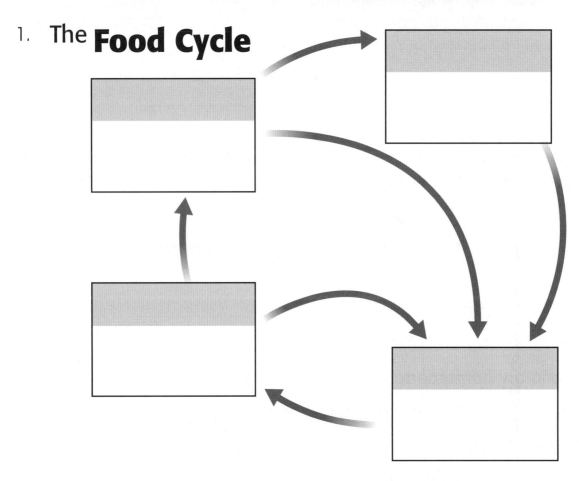

2.   What do the arrows of the food cycle represent?

   _____

3.   Can some animals be both primary and secondary consumers? Explain.

   _____

   _____

C. Fill in the blanks with the given words to complete the paragraph and label the energy pyramid with the words in bold. Then answer the question.

As energy is transferred from one 1._____ to another, some energy is lost. Only a small amount of an organism's energy is transferred in a 2._____ ; therefore, an ecosystem needs more of the eaten than the 3._____ . The higher up an organism is in the food chain, the 4._____ its population.

organism
smaller
food chain
eaters

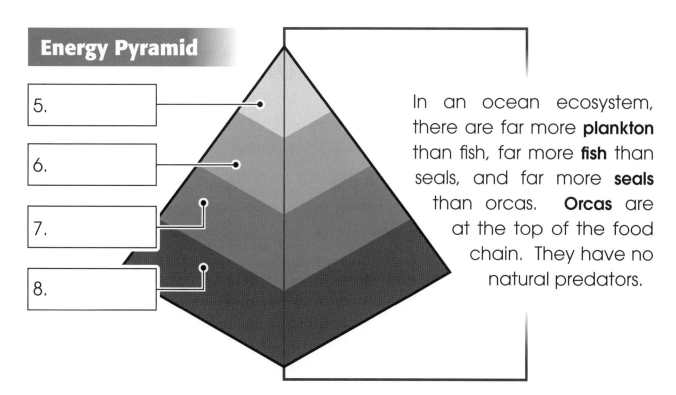

Energy Pyramid

5.

6.

7.

8.

In an ocean ecosystem, there are far more **plankton** than fish, far more **fish** than seals, and far more **seals** than orcas. **Orcas** are at the top of the food chain. They have no natural predators.

9. A new pod of orcas has come to an area where another pod already lives. Describe what might happen to the animals in the energy pyramid if they stay.

_____

_____

D. Read the passage. Then answer the questions.

This is our home.

The Return of
Wolves to
Yellowstone National Park

Yellowstone National Park in the United States was once home to a large population of wolves. Ranchers who settled in the area, however, considered wolves to be a nuisance, as wolves hunted cattle and other livestock; by the 1920s, all of the wolves in the area had been killed.

By the 1960s, the elk population in the area was critically high due to a lack of predators. Since elk are primary consumers that eat large amounts of plant matter, their overpopulation was threatening the plant life in the area. This threat to plant life had an adverse effect on many other animal species, which lost sources of food and shelter. Scientists planned for the reintroduction of wolves to the area in order to restore balance to the ecosystem, but it took many years to set the plan in motion.

It was not until the 1990s that scientists reintroduced wolves to Yellowstone National Park, when 66 wolves were released into the area. The reintroduction was considered a success since pups were born and wolf packs were formed. The wolves immediately began to control the elk population which, in turn, meant that both the variety of plant life and the populations of animal species that had been in danger increased. The return of the ecosystem's top consumer returned balance to the ecosystem.

1. Match the graphs with the correct titles. Then label the axes.

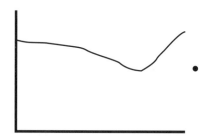

•

Species in
Yellowstone National Park

• Wolf Population

• Plant Population

• Elk Population

•

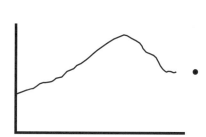

•

2. Use an energy pyramid to show the relationships among **wolves**, **elk**, and **plants**. Then describe what happened when the wolves were removed from the pyramid.

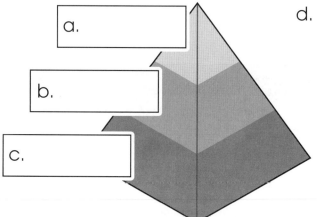

a.

b.

c.

d. When the wolves were removed from the pyramid...

_____

_____

_____

_____ .

3 Cycles in the Environment

The existing amounts of oxygen, water, nitrogen, and carbon on Earth are all that we will ever have access to. If matter could not be recycled, they would have run out a long time ago. In this unit, you will see how matter cycles in the environment.

Oxygen Cycle

carbon dioxide

oxygen

After completing this unit, you will

- understand the cycles of matter in the environment.

- understand how cycled matter promotes sustainability in an ecosystem.

Ted, we are a big part of the oxygen cycle!

Vocabulary

matter: physical substance that takes up space and has mass

sustainability: the ability of an ecosystem to endure

combustion: burning

an example of combustion:
campfire

Crop rotation is a farming method in which farmers rotate different crops in a field to keep the soil rich in nutrients. For example, many legumes, such as beans, have bacteria that replenish the soil with nitrogen – something all plants need but none can produce. Hence, one season, a legume might be planted, and the next season, a grain, such as corn, might be planted. The grain uses the nitrogen in the soil, and the legume's bacteria replenish it. Crop rotation is an example of people manipulating a natural cycle.

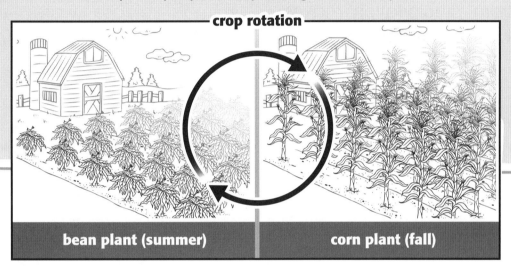

crop rotation

bean plant (summer) | **corn plant (fall)**

A. Read about the oxygen cycle. Label the diagram with the words in bold.

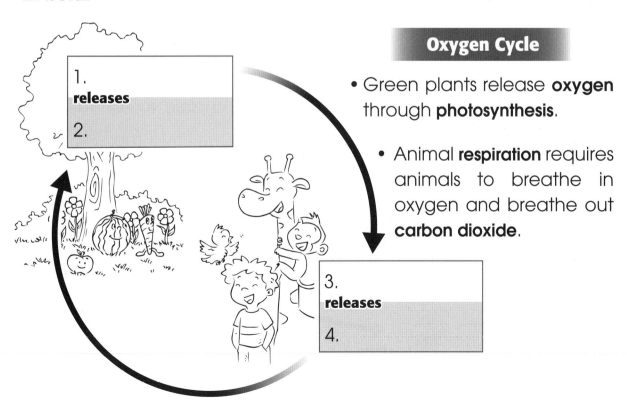

1.
releases
2.

3.
releases
4.

Oxygen Cycle

- Green plants release **oxygen** through **photosynthesis**.

- Animal **respiration** requires animals to breathe in oxygen and breathe out **carbon dioxide**.

B. Match the terms in the diagram with their descriptions.

1. _____

The sun's heat causes water to turn to vapour.

2. _____

Water falls from clouds into lakes, oceans, rivers, and onto the ground.

3. _____

Water from precipitation makes its way back to the ocean.

4. _____

Animals release water vapour into the air.

5. _____

Plants release water vapour into the air.

6. _____

Water vapour in the atmosphere cools and forms clouds.

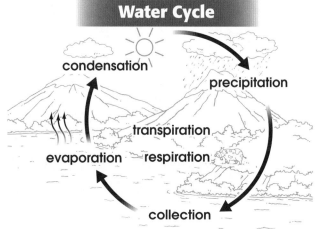

Water Cycle

condensation

precipitation

transpiration

evaporation   respiration

collection

C. Fill in the blanks with the words in the diagram.

Nitrogen Cycle

animals

waste

air

plants

bacteria

Nitrogen is the most abundant gas in the atmosphere. 1._____ need it to live and grow, but they are unable to use the nitrogen in the air. 2._____ in the soil, however, are able to "fix" nitrogen, which means they can make it usable to plants. Then 3._____ eat plants. As bacteria work to decompose organisms and their 4._____ , they return nitrogen to the 5._____ .

D. Read about carbon. Then match the terms in the diagram with the correct descriptions.

Carbon is found in all living things, as well as in water, rocks, soil, and air. Pairing up with oxygen to form carbon dioxide (CO_2), it cycles through the ecosystem in a number of ways.

When people burn fossil fuels, they release carbon dioxide, which would otherwise have remained in the ground, into the air. This alters carbon's natural cycle and negatively impacts the environment.

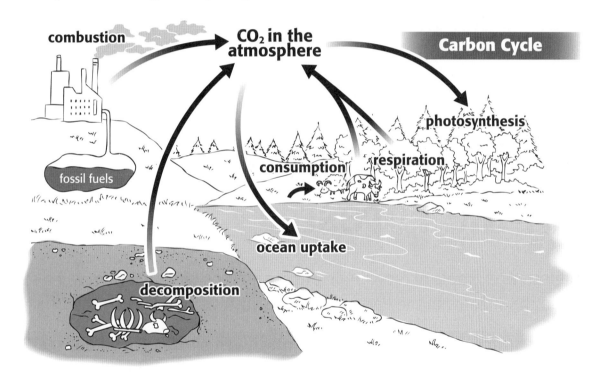

1. _____ : from the atmosphere to plants

2. _____ : from living things to the atmosphere

3. _____ : from organic matter to the atmosphere

4. _____ : from fossil fuels to the atmosphere when fuels are burned

5. _____ : from the atmosphere to the oceans

6. _____ : from plants to animals

E.   Read the passage. Then answer the questions.

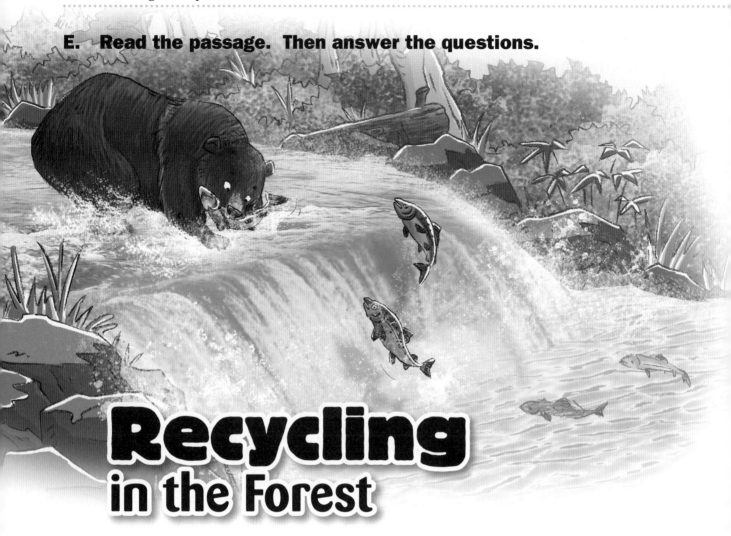

Recycling
in the Forest

An interesting example of recycling matter in an ecosystem happens when salmon spawn in the streams of the Pacific coast in British Columbia.

Beginning in late summer, salmon return to their birth stream from the Pacific Ocean, swimming upstream against strong currents until they find the perfect spot to lay and fertilize their eggs. Their journey is extremely difficult, and the salmon are so exhausted after completing it that they die within days of spawning. However, their bodies live on. The substances of which they are made, their building blocks, are broken down and recycled in the environment.

Salmon left in the stream sink to the stream bed; bears lumber into the stream and carry salmon onto the shore, eating some and leaving some. Other animals do the same. All of these animals will then deposit what they have eaten in the forest as waste. Wherever the salmon end up, and however they get there, decomposers will do their part to break them down into nutrients, which will become the building blocks of other plants and animals.

1. Look at the pictures. Describe how recycling happens in the forest starting with the life of a salmon.

Recycling in the Forest

Ⓐ _____

_____

Ⓑ _____

_____

Ⓒ _____

_____

Ⓓ _____

_____

2. What is the purpose of the salmon's return from the Pacific Ocean to their birth stream?

_____

3. What happens to salmon after they lay and fertilize their eggs?

_____

4. What does the term "building blocks" mean in the passage?

_____

Introduction

Among decomposers, yeast is one we are familiar with in the kitchen. Yeast uses food to grow, and as it grows, it changes the characteristics of the food it is using; it decomposes it. We use yeast to make bread because it turns sugar into gas; the gas makes our bread light and fluffy.

> *Does food exposed to yeast decompose at a different rate than food that isn't?*

Food exposed to yeast will decompose at _____ rate than food not exposed to yeast.

(a faster/a slower)

Steps

1. Cut two small slices of the banana. They should be of equal size.

2. Peel the two slices and make sure they do not have brown spots on them.

Materials

- *a banana*
- *2 sealable sandwich bags*
- *water*
- *baker's yeast*
- *a knife*
- *a tablespoon*
- *a marker*

3.   Place one slice in each bag.

4.   Measure and pour one tablespoon of water in each bag.

5.   Add a large pinch of yeast to only one bag.

6.   Seal the bags and write "yeast" on the one containing yeast.

7.   Place both bags near a sunny window.

Day		

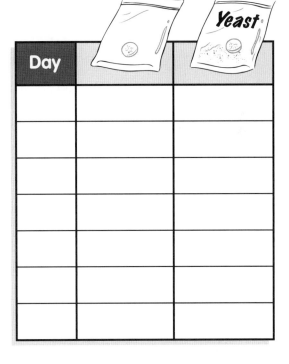

8.   Observe the bags for a week and record your observations in the chart.

Result

Which sample decomposed faster?

_____

Conclusion

The hypothesis was: _____

_____

My experiment _____ the hypothesis.
                      supported/did not support

4 Stability and Change in Ecosystems

We do not usually see major changes in an ecosystem. In our lifetimes, ecosystems appear stable. Indeed, they are kept stable by limiting factors, both biotic and abiotic. In this unit, you will see how ecosystems stay the same, and how they go through changes called succession.

After completing this unit, you will

- understand that succession occurs naturally over time.
- know the difference between primary and secondary succession.
- understand that limiting factors help control an ecosystem.

It will take a very long time for a new ecosystem to develop here.

Vocabulary

succession: the gradual replacement of one habitat with another

factor: something that causes or contributes to a result

annual plant: plant that lives for only one year

perennial plant: plant that lives for many years

example of a perennial plant: **tulips**

Scientists count species populations in order to study the health of an ecosystem. However, it is hard to count every member of a species, so they use a method called random sampling to count a species' population. Random sampling helps estimate totals when a population is large and evenly distributed.

Random Sampling Steps

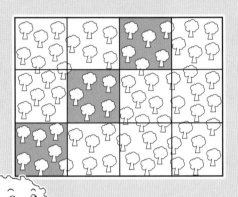

1. Divide an area into a grid (12 squares in this grid).

2. Pick a few samples and count the members of a species therein (3 samples: contain 7 trees, 6 trees, and 5 trees).

3. Find the total of the samples and the average for the samples (18 trees in total; 6 trees each on average).

4. Predict the population by multiplying the average with the total number of squares (6 x 12 = 72 trees).

There are about 72 trees.

A. Fill in the blanks with the given words. Then number the pictures in the correct order.

slowly   plants   adaptations   extinction

Succession is the normal progression or change in the types of 1._____ and animals in an ecosystem. It happens 2._____ over years. It may lead to the 3._____ of species that do not adapt to changes in the ecosystem. It stimulates 4._____ in other plants and animals so that they can continue to thrive.

Succession in a Pond

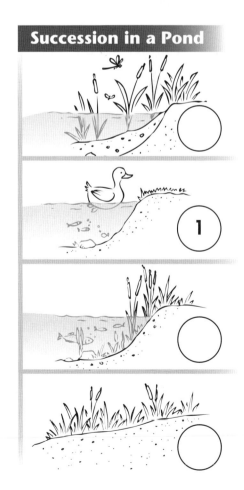

B. Complete the descriptions of succession. Then write 1 to 5 to put the stages of an example of secondary succession in order.

| fire | volcanic eruption | hurricane | flood | newly exposed rock |
| agriculture | climate change | paved areas | logging | landslide |

1. Primary succession occurs in places where there is no **air / soil** and **no / some** life exists; it is the gradual **growth / reduction** of an ecosystem.

Conditions that allow for primary succession include:

_____

2. Secondary succession occurs in places where there is **lots of / no** soil and where **river / life** has existed or exists; it is the gradual **replacement / spread** of one ecosystem with another.

Events that trigger secondary succession include:

_____

3.

Succession after a Forest Fire

Example of **Secondary Succession**

◯ Sprouting seeds appear above the ground; mosses grow in the cracks in rocks.

◯ Larger, taller, and longer-lived trees begin to grow.

◯ Burned trees, and dry, bare ground are all that is left.

◯ Richer soil supports the growth of large shrubs, small trees, and perennial plants.

◯ Grasses, small shrubs, and annual plants grow and produce seeds.

C. Circle the correct answers and write whether the limiting factors in the ecosystems are "biotic" or "abiotic". Then answer the question.

A limiting factor helps **feed / control** populations and **increases / decreases** stability in an ecosystem.

Limiting Factors

1. available food

_____

2. number of predators

_____

3. available space

_____

4. Spawning salmon need...

a. dissolved oxygen.

_____

b. shade.

_____

c. clean, clear water.

_____

d. a riverbed of gravel.

_____

5. Write one biotic limiting factor and one abiotic limiting factor in the ecosystem of a large city park.

a biotic limiting factor: _____

an abiotic limiting factor: _____

D. Read the passage. Then answer the questions.

Surtsey:
a "Baby" Island and Ecosystem

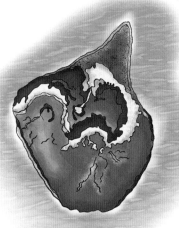

bird's-eye view of Surtsey

Surtsey is an island 32 kilometres off the southern coast of Iceland that formed as a result of oceanic volcanic eruptions between 1963 and 1967. Though Surtsey began as a hunk of volcanic rock, an ecosystem rapidly developed and is still developing on the island. What makes Surtsey fascinating is that ecological succession is occurring without human interference. The only people allowed on the island are scientists, whose purpose is to study it; therefore, succession on Surtsey has been carefully documented.

Succession on Surtsey began with the growth of bacteria and fungi. Within a few years, mosses and lichens began to grow in cracks in the volcanic rock. Very slowly, they formed soil by breaking down rock and fertilizing it with plant matter. Seeds floated to Surtsey on ocean currents, and hardy plants grew in the tiny patches of soil. As plant materials for nesting became available, sea birds such as gulls ventured to the island to nest, dispersing more seeds and fertilizing the soil with their waste. More plants grew as a result, which meant more sea birds came to nest. Insects arrived by sea, wind, and on birds, and marine life developed around the island. Large populations of seals now use the island as a breeding ground and their main ocean predator, the orca, is a resident of its shores.

1. Label the map to show the location of "Iceland" and "Surtsey". Then write the information.

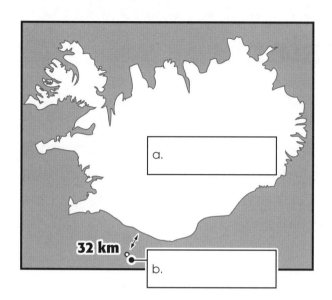

a.

32 km

b.

Formation of Surtsey Island

When: _____

How: _____

What Makes Surtsey Island Amazing:

_____

_____

_____

2. Put the succession of Surtsey in order. Write 1 to 4.

bacteria   small plants   mosses

3. Check the living things that may be found on Surtsey.

(A) maple trees   (B) flies   (C) monkeys

(D) seals   (E) grass   (F) mites

(G) anteaters   (H) ostriches   (I) gulls

4. Why is human activity restricted on Surtsey Island?

_____

_____

5 Human Activities and Ecosystems

Many of our activities alter the balance of the ecosystems we inhabit. Our practices and technologies help us, but they can be detrimental to an ecosystem. In this unit, you will look at ways we alter the balance of and interactions within an ecosystem.

After completing this unit, you will

- know the difference between a practice and a technology.

- understand how human activities and technologies alter the balance and interactions in the environment.

The poisonous waste from the factories upriver is harming the river ecosystem!

black bear native to Ontario

Vocabulary

native species: a species that naturally lives in an area

fish stocks: the population of a species of fish in a given area

wetlands: lands that are saturated with water, such as marshes and swamps

watershed: an area of land in which water from rain or melting snow drains downward into the same body of water

In the garden, we alter the ecosystem by removing some plants and planting others. Sometimes we even remove native plants and plant non-native ones. We add nutrients and water to the soil, and even add more soil. We encourage the presence of some animals, such as earthworms, bees, and hummingbirds, while discouraging others, such as slugs and beetles. We create new ecosystems and control them. Try observing a garden and then observing an area that is mostly untouched by people, such as a conservation area, to see the differences between the two.

A. Sort the practices and technologies into the correct categories.

Practices and Technologies

crop rotation: different crops are grown on a section of land at different times

skidder: vehicle that removes cut trees from the forest

trolling: using lines and bait to catch fish

inorganic fertilizer: fertilizer made of synthetic chemicals

clear-cutting: cutting down all the trees in an area

trawler: boat that drags a net through the sea

Fishing

practice:

_____

technology:

_____

Farming

practice:

_____

technology:

_____

Logging

practice:

_____

technology:

_____

B. Match the human activities with the effects they have on ecosystems. Write the activities and circle the correct words. Then write the effect of mining on an ecosystem.

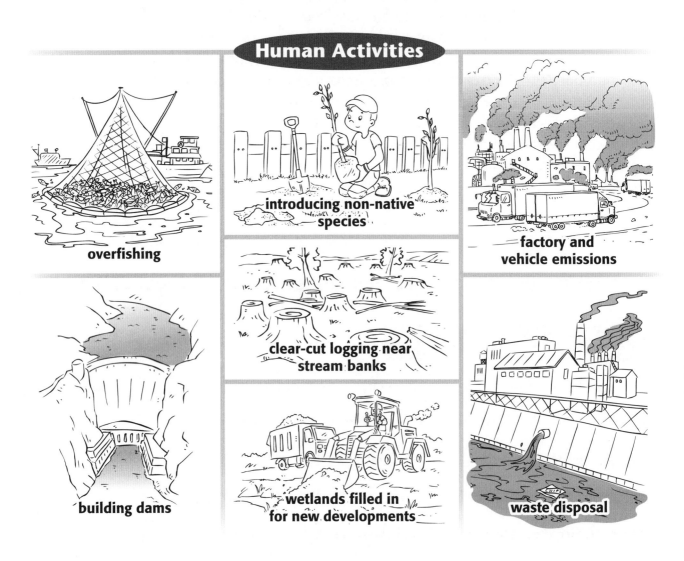

Effects of Human Activities on Ecosystems

1. _____

   Effect: It increases competition for native species so that they are
   less / more likely to thrive.

2. _____

   Effect: Waste can leach into soil and water, thereby
   polluting / enhancing ecosystems.

3. _____

   Effect: It depletes fish stocks, which results in **less / more** diversity
   within a species, or even **growth / extinction** of a species.

4. _____

   Effect: It destroys animal and plant habitats, and **removes / adds**
   a natural filter in a watershed.

5. _____

   Effect: A lack of trees causes soil **build-up / erosion** , which results
   in too much silt getting into the stream.

6. _____

   Effect: They pollute the air that animals, including humans, breathe,
   and cause **acid rain / frost** that harms plants.

7. _____

   Effect: Sediment, and the nutrients in the sediment, can no
   longer flow to the estuary, as the flow of water is
   disrupted / increased .

8. **Mining**

   Effect:_____

   _____

   _____

   _____

C. Read the passage. Then answer the questions.

Human activities damage ecosystems, but they can also restore them. One way to restore them is to plant trees. Trees help ecosystems and people in many ways: they "store" the harmful carbon we release when we burn fossil fuels, enhance biodiversity, create habitats, provide shade for people, animals, and other plants, provide fuel for people around the world, prevent soil erosion and flooding, and are a key resource in the economies of many communities.

In 2007, the United Nations Environment Programme (UNEP) started a project called "Plant for the Planet: Billion Tree Campaign". Its goal is to encourage individuals, communities, youth organizations, businesses, and governments to plant one billion trees around the world each year. In order for the project to benefit an area and its people, UNEP suggests that a variety of species be planted, and that the trees planted should be native to the area. The project's website claims that over ten billion trees have been planted in 170 countries since 2007! The Ontario government is one of many governments committed to UNEP's mission: its goal is to plant, and to encourage Ontarians to plant, 50 million trees by 2020.

You can participate too! Ask your teacher or parents about planting trees in your community, and report your tree planting to UNEP's website.

Plant a Tree!

1. Check the ways trees benefit ecosystems and people. Then write one more benefit.

Trees...

(A) provide us with steel products.

(B) provide habitats and shade for people, animals, and other plants.

(C) provide us with food and numerous products.

(D) produce water.

(E) provide soil stabilization and erosion control.

(F) store carbon and clean the atmosphere.

(✔) _____

2. What project was undertaken by the UNEP in 2007? What is its goal?

_____

_____

_____

3. Why does the UNEP suggest planting trees that are native to the area?

_____

_____

4. Suggest a kind of tree that should be planted in each of these places. Do some research to help you make your choice.

a. Toronto: b. Vancouver:

_____   _____

c. Moshi, Tanzania: d. Shikoku, Japan:

_____   _____

6 Controlling Human Impacts

We can make positive impacts on the environment. Large efforts can be seen on a national level through government policies and laws. Smaller efforts are just as important, and often initiate larger efforts. In this unit, you will examine some of the actions we take to minimize our negative impacts on ecosystems.

Mom, look how beautiful the butterfly weed is! I'm so happy we reintroduced this native species to our garden.

After completing this unit, you will

- know some of the ways governments and organizations protect ecosystems.

- understand that there are many things each one of us can do to have a positive impact on the environment.

butterfly weed

well: an access to groundwater

Vocabulary

intervention: an action taken to prevent or cause an outcome

reintroduction: releasing a native species into the wild

groundwater: fresh water below the ground; important source of drinking water

An Aboriginal perspective on ecological responsibility is to use nature without waste. Traditional uses of the Western red cedar tree are in line with this idea, as demonstrated in the chart.

We can be ecologically responsible in ways that follow this perspective by reducing the amount of waste we produce.

Western Red Cedar Tree	Use
trunk	canoes, buildings
branches	baskets, ropes
roots	nets
bark	clothes, mats

The next time you go shopping, think about ways you can reduce your waste by choosing items that have little or no packaging.

A. Match each Canadian environmental intervention program with its description. Write the letter.

Intervention Programs

1. fire management
2. native species reintroduction
3. wildlife corridor
4. national and provincial parks
5. captive breeding
6. COSEWIC

A. preserving and protecting ecosystems

B. preventing or controlling forest fires

C. allowing the natural movement of wildlife without interruption

D. breeding endangered animals to increase populations, sometimes for reintroduction into the wild

E. replacing non-native plants with species native to an ecosystem

F. Committee on the Status of Endangered Wildlife in Canada; putting plants and animals in categories such as threatened or endangered

B. Read what the Rivers family say. Then read about the negative impacts of human activities on the environment and write what the Rivers have done to reduce these impacts.

The Rivers family have become more environmentally responsible.

My wife and I walk to work instead of driving.

I buy food for my family from a local farmers' market instead of a supermarket, which means that the food did not have to travel far to get to the dinner table.

In the washroom, we have installed a device on the toilet that reduces the amount of water used each time it is flushed.

I ride my bicycle to school instead of being driven.

I'll help plant some native plants in the backyard.

Human Activities

1. **Problem 1**   We overuse groundwater, and it is not easily replaced.

   Rivers' Solution: _____

   _____

2. **Problem 2**   We introduce non-native species that threaten native species.

   Rivers' Solution: _____

   _____

3. **Problem 3**   We drive cars and trucks that cause air pollution and acid rain.

   Rivers' Solution: _____

   _____

C. **Write the meaning of each of the three Rs – reduce, reuse, and recycle. Match each example with the correct R and write an example of your own for each. Then answer the question.**

Examples of the Three Rs ▬▬▬▬▬▬▬▬▬▬▬

- *giving clothes you have outgrown to others*
- *turning the heat down and wearing a sweater*
- *returning all recyclable materials properly*

Following the three Rs is a great way to be environmentally responsible!

The Three Rs

1. To **Reduce** Means: _____

   Example: _____

   My Example: _____

2. To **Reuse** Means: _____

   Example: _____

   My Example: _____

3. To **Recycle** Means: _____

   Example: _____

   My Example: _____

4.
   Manufacturing with recycled materials can be more difficult or costly than making the same objects with raw materials.

   Why is the "Reduce, Reuse, Recycle" slogan in that particular order?

   _____

   _____

D. Read the passage. Then complete the chart. (You will have to do some research in order to complete it.)

Protecting the Environment:
Efforts at all Levels

The government of Canada protects ecosystems in many ways. For instance, Parks Canada manages national parks, which are protected by law that includes a ban on logging or mining in national parks, and the restriction of camping to certain areas.

Provincial governments protect ecosystems as well. The Ontario Ministry of Natural Resources (MNR), for example, decides what animals can be hunted, and where, when, and how many can be hunted. For example, the wild turkey can only be hunted between specific dates in the spring and fall, and only one to two birds can be hunted per season. These regulations protect the ecosystem by controlling populations and ensure that the diversity of species is not threatened.

Cities and towns protect the environment, too. The City of Toronto regulates waste disposal, maintains city parks, and creates programs to encourage the use of environmentally friendly modes of the transportation, like bicycles. An example of a city bylaw that protects the environment is that drivers are not allowed to leave their vehicles idling.

Your school may also have rules that protect the environment. Maybe you are not allowed to take packaging to the playground, or you are encouraged to pick up litter in the schoolyard.

| Parks Canada |

(www.pc.gc.ca)

Federal
Government

| 3. |

another department that focuses on the natural environment

Two of its Duties:

1. _____

_____

_____

2. _____

_____

_____

Two of its Duties:

4. _____

_____

_____

5. _____

_____

_____

CANADA

Provincial
Government

| 6. |

name of the department

What the department does to manage

- hunting: 7. _____

_____

_____

_____

- parks: 8. _____

_____

_____

Municipal
Government

| 9. |

name of the city

What the city does to protect the environment:

10. _____

11. _____

12. _____

| 13. |

name of your community

What you do to protect the environment:

14. _____

_____

Introduction

Most garbage decomposes eventually, but some materials decompose quickly under the right circumstances, that is, with the help of water, air, soil bacteria, and other organisms. They are called biodegradable materials and should be composted instead of being sent to landfills. Many other materials take a long, long time to decompose.

Which of the materials we throw out will take a long, long time to decompose?

Hypothesis

Fill in the blanks with these four choices: foil, plastic, paper, apple.

_____ are biodegradable, while _____ are not.

Steps

1. Fill the jars with equal amounts of soil.

2. Place the apple pieces in one jar and cover them with the soil. Then label it.

apple

Materials

- **4 clean jam jars**
- **3 small pieces each of an apple, a paper bag, aluminum foil, and a plastic lid**
- **soil**

3. Repeat step 2 with the paper bag, aluminum foil, and plastic pieces.

4. Place the jars side by side, with lids placed loosely on top (so that air can still get in), in a safe spot.

5. Sprinkle water on the soil every few days to keep the soil moist.

6. Observe the materials for two months. Record your observations (e.g. any change in size or colour or texture) in a chart like the one shown.

Date	apple	paper	foil	plastic

Result

1. Which materials:
   - decomposed?   _____
   - did not decompose?   _____

2. What do the results tell you about how you should dispose of waste (e.g. about recycling, composting, reducing)?

_____

_____

Conclusion

The hypothesis was: _____

_____

My experiment _____ the hypothesis.

supported/did not support

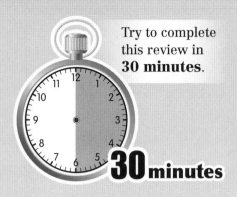

Try to complete this review in **30 minutes**.

30 minutes

This review consists of five sections, from A to E. The marks for each question are shown in parentheses. The circle at the bottom right corner is for the marks you get in each section. An overall record is on the last page of the review.

A. Write T for true and F for false.

1. Producers are at the top of all energy pyramids. **(2)** _____

2. Nitrogen-fixing bacteria are bacteria that turn nitrogen into a form that plants can use. **(2)** _____

3. "Community" is a term used to describe an ecosystem's living members. **(2)** _____

4. Arrows in a food cycle represent water transfer between organisms. **(2)** _____

5. Abiotic elements do not play an important role in an ecosystem. **(2)**

    _____

6. Both plants and animals contribute to the oxygen cycle. **(2)**

    _____

12

B. Do the matching.

1.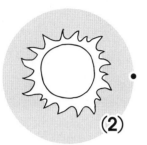
   (2)

2.
   (2)

3.
   (2)

4.
   (2)

5.
   (2)

6.
   (2)

- biotic element in a desert ecosystem

- human activity that depletes fish stocks

- abiotic limiting factor for plant growth

- a mode of transportation that minimizes our impact on the environment

- interaction between biotic and abiotic elements in a river ecosystem

- human activity that causes acid rain

C. Name the models of energy transfer and complete each model with the given words. Then answer the questions.

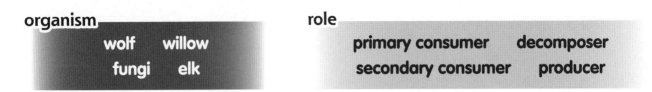

organism
wolf   willow
fungi   elk

role
primary consumer   decomposer
secondary consumer   producer

1. model: _____ **(2)**

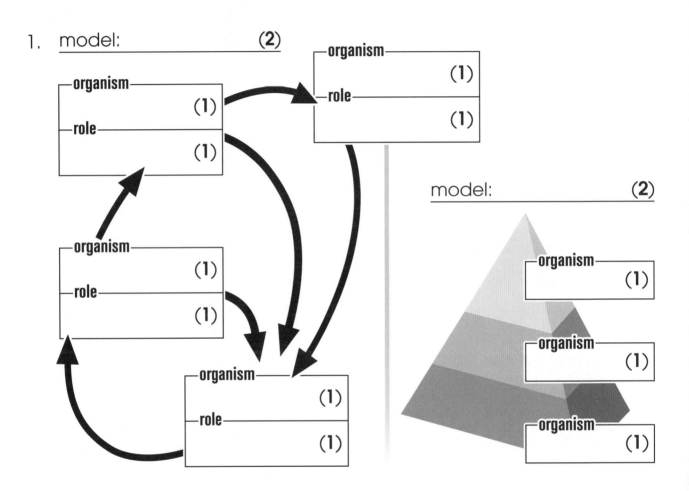

─organism─
    (1)
─role──────
    (1)

─organism─
    (1)
─role──────
    (1)

─organism─
    (1)
─role──────
    (1)

─organism─
    (1)
─role──────
    (1)

model: _____ **(2)**

─organism─
    (1)

─organism─
    (1)

─organism─
    (1)

2. Which model better represents

    a. the recycling of nutrients?

    _____ **(2)**

    b. energy loss during energy transfer?

    _____ **(2)**

3. Name one biotic limiting factor and one abiotic limiting factor for the elk population.

    a. biotic: _____ **(2)**

    b. abiotic: _____ **(2)**

4. What larger ecosystem might this forest be a part of?

    _____ **(3)**

5. The willow's interaction with abiotic elements in the ecosystem is essential for the survival of other living things. Name and describe this interaction. **(5)**

_____

_____

6a. What would happen to the other organisms if the wolf population decreased? **(5)**

_____

_____

b. Name two actions a government could take to restore balance to the ecosystem if this change were to take place. **(4)**

_____

7. Long ago, this forest was a farm field.

a. Name the process that turned the abandoned farm into a forest. **(3)**

_____

b. Name two events that could trigger the forest's replacement with another ecosystem. **(2)**

_____

c. What is the process of the ecosystem growth on Surtsey Island? How is it different from the process that turned a field into a forest? **(5)**

_____

_____

_____

_____

50

D. Label the components involved in the carbon cycle. Then answer the question.

respiration   combustion   atmosphere   ocean uptake
consumption   photosynthesis   fossil fuels   decomposition

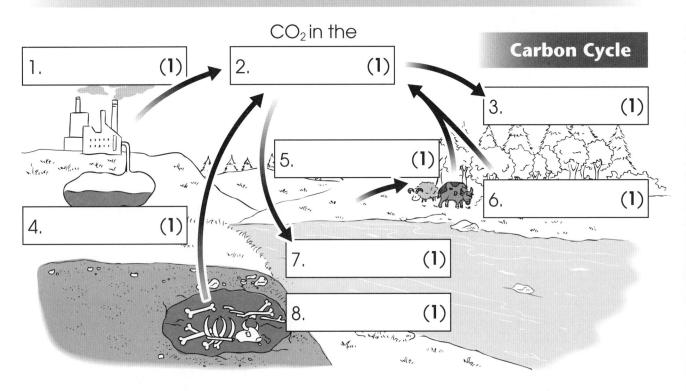

CO$_2$ in the

Carbon Cycle

1. _____ (1)
2. _____ (1)
3. _____ (1)
4. _____ (1)
5. _____ (1)
6. _____ (1)
7. _____ (1)
8. _____ (1)

9. How is the cycling of matter essential to the sustainability of ecosystems? Write another example of a natural cycle. **(6)**

_____

_____

14

E. Answer the questions.

1. Explain the significance of the order of the three Rs. **(6)**

_____

_____

2. How can shopping at a local market instead of a supermarket reduce our negative impact on the environment? **(6)**

_____

_____

12

My Record

Section A	12
Section B	12
Section C	50
Section D	14
Section E	12

Total

100

80-100

Great work! You really understand your science stuff! Research your favourite science topics at the library or on the Internet to find out more about the topics related to this section. Keep challenging yourself to learn more!

60-79

Good work! You understand some basic concepts, but try reading through the units again to see whether you can master the material! Go over the questions that you had trouble with to make sure you know the correct answers.

below 60

You can do much better! Try reading over the units again. Ask your parents or teachers any questions you might have. Once you feel confident that you know the material, try the review again. Science is exciting, so don't give up!

The Environmentalist

Thanks to the efforts of environmentalists, more and more people are aware of the importance of conserving natural resources and ecosystems and preventing them from damage caused by human activities such as logging, mining, hunting, and fishing.

David Suzuki is one of the most respected environmentalists in Canada. Through his books, talks, radio and TV programs, as well as his David Suzuki Foundation, Suzuki has been able to reach many Canadians, young and old, and educate them on "living healthier, more fulfilled and just lives with tips on building Earth-friendly infrastructure, making smart energy choices, using efficient transportation, and being mindful of the products, food and water we use". He has also been working hard to ensure that "Canada is doing its fair share to avoid dangerous climate change and to protect the diversity and health of Canada's marine, freshwater, and terrestrial creatures and ecosystems".

Because of his contributions to protecting the environment, Suzuki was awarded a United Nations Environment Program Medal in 1987, and in an exclusive Reader's Digest poll conducted in 2010, Suzuki was voted as the most trusted Canadian.

Cool Science Facts

1 Fish never close their eyes. Do they sleep at all?

2 Do small animals or large animals live longer?

3 How are antlers and horns different?

4 What is in insect repellents that keeps insects away?

5 Green leaves have green chlorophyll to make food through photosynthesis. How do plants without green leaves make food?

Find the answers on the next page.

Cool Science Facts

1 Fish do sleep, but because they have no eyelids, they sleep with their eyes open. When asleep, some of them float motionless in place and some float near the bottom of the sea or tanks. Some deep ocean fish even appear to stay moving while sleeping, which is probably because they have to keep water and oxygen flowing through their gills for breathing.

Guys, wake up. It's time to play.

2 Larger animals tend to live longer because of their slower heart rates in general. Mice, for example, have heart rates of 500 beats per minute, whereas cats have heart rates that are about one fourth of that at 120 beats per minute. As a result, cats live about 16 years, that is 4 times as long as mice, which live about 4 years. Turtles' hearts beat much slower than that of mice and cats. That is why they live such long lives.

4

Some insects, such as mosquitoes, are attracted to odours emitted by the human skin and carbon dioxide from breath. Insect repellents work by giving off a scent that insects typically avoid or by masking the alluring human scent, making a person unattractive for feeding.

5

Though some leaves are not green, they photosynthesize with the traces of green chlorophyll embedded in them.

reddish leaves

Bloodgood Japanese Maple

3

Antlers and horns are both bony structures that grow out from the frontals of the skull of animals. However, unlike antlers, horns are permanent and never stop growing whereas antlers are shed every year. Also, antlers branch out but horns never do.

antler

horn

Section 2

Understanding Structures and Mechanisms

Scan this QR code or go to Download Centre at *www.popularbook.ca* for some fun scientific explorations!

EXPLORATION 1 **Spring Force**
Investigate spring force using elastic bands.

EXPLORATION 2 **Where is the centre of gravity?**
Examine the concept of centre of gravity.

1 Basic Structures

Structures can be human-made or they can occur in nature. In this unit, you will examine the three basic forms of structures. You will begin to recognize that different forms provide structures with different functions, but that structures with similar functions do not always have similar forms, and vice versa.

After completing this unit, you will

- understand that structures are classified as frame, shell, or solid structures.

- understand that structures with similar functions may have different forms.

- understand that some structures are mixtures of the three basic forms.

Mom, all flowers have similar functions, but their forms can be very different.

Vocabulary

structure: something with a definite shape and size

form: the shape of something

function: what something is used for

form: small; like a net
function: catches prey

Extension

Structures are either natural or human-made. There are many human-made structures that resemble natural structures. Think of what an arch bridge looks like. Did you know that our bodies have natural arch structures which are similar to arch bridges? Have you ever climbed a dome frame structure in a park? Did you know that the design of the frame looks like the homes of some animals?

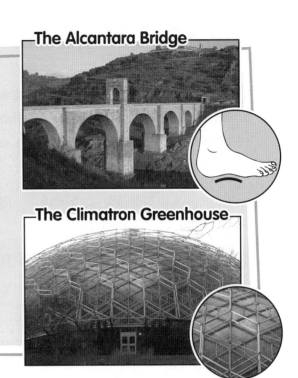

The Alcantara Bridge

The Climatron Greenhouse

A. Match each natural structure with the human-made structure that has a similar form. Then answer the questions.

1. **Human-made Structure**

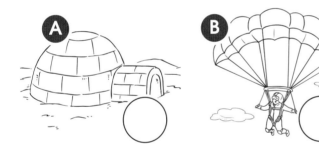

A

B

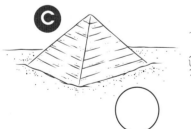

C

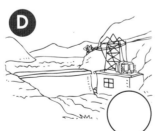

D

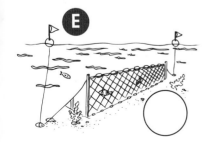

E

F

Natural Structure

P tulip

Q turtle shell

R sand dune

S spiderweb

T beaver dam

U dandelion seed

2. Which pairs are similar in function as well as form?

_____

3. Do structures of the same form always have a similar function?

_____

B. **Match the three basic forms of structures with their descriptions. Sort the examples into the correct kinds of structures. Then write one more example of each.**

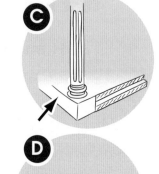

| frame | shell | solid |

Three Basic Forms of Structures

1. [　　　　　]

    one solid piece or solid pieces piled together

    • Examples: _____ , _____ , _____

    • My example: _____

2. [　　　　　]

    a framework of connected parts, usually bars or beams

    • Examples: _____ , _____ , _____

    • My example: _____

3. [　　　　　]

    a panel or connected panels, usually for the purpose of protecting or holding

    • Examples: _____ , _____ , _____

    • My example: _____

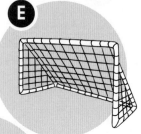

C. Name the two different forms that are in each structure. Then name the structure and give examples of structures of your own.

Forms of Structures: **frame   shell   solid**

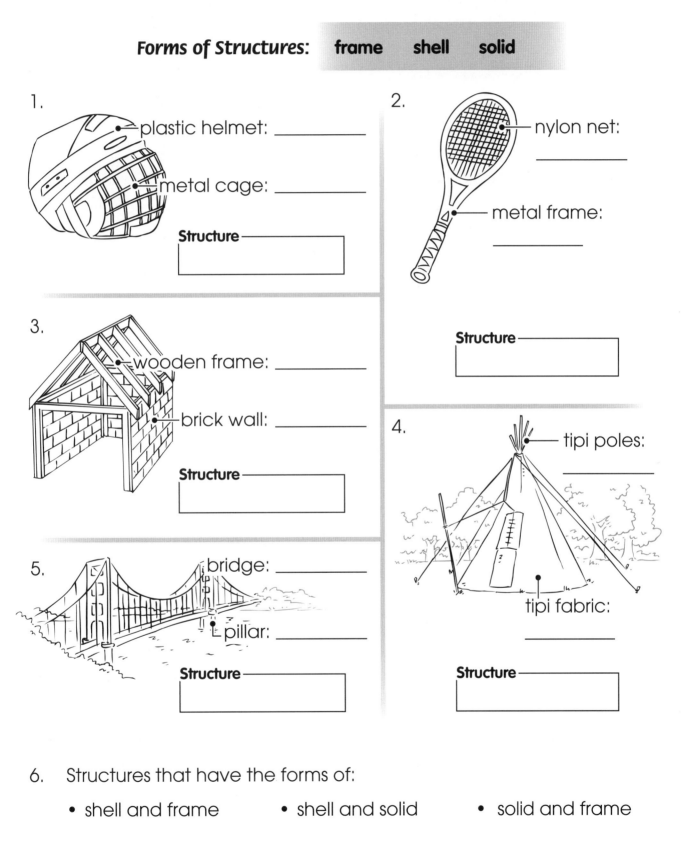

1.
plastic helmet: _____

metal cage: _____

Structure _____

2.
nylon net:

_____

metal frame:

_____

Structure _____

3.
wooden frame: _____

brick wall: _____

Structure _____

4.
tipi poles:

_____

tipi fabric:

_____

Structure _____

5.
bridge: _____

pillar: _____

Structure _____

6. Structures that have the forms of:

• shell and frame   • shell and solid   • solid and frame

_____   _____   _____

D. **Read the passage. Describe the three forms of structures. Then name the form of each structure.**

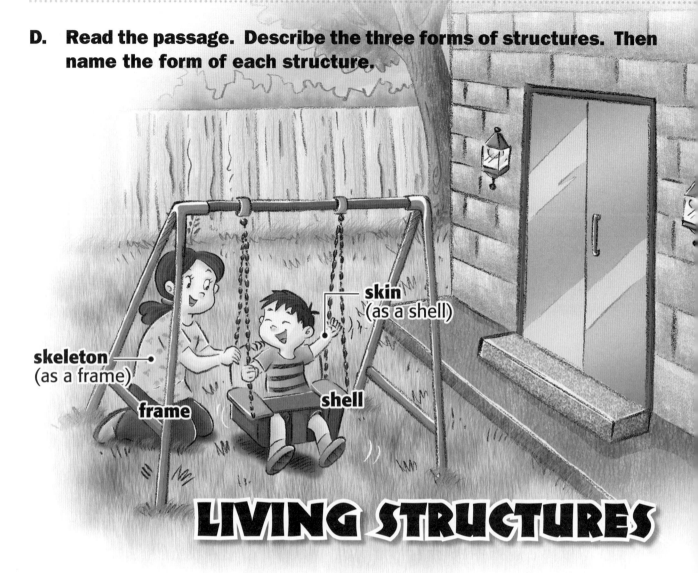

Structures are not just the inanimate objects made in nature or by people. Living things are structures, too, with specific forms and functions.

Each plant in your neighbourhood began as a tiny seed covered in a shell whose purpose was to protect it until it germinated, much like a helmet is a shell structure that protects your head. A living tree has a strong trunk that is a solid structure, and branches that form a frame. The eggs from which birds, reptiles, and amphibians hatch are incredibly strong shell structures that protect the baby animals inside until they are fully developed.

Even your own body is a structure made up of many smaller structures. Your skin is a shell that protects your insides and holds them all tightly together; your skeleton is a frame that gives shape to your insides; your teeth and your nails are solid structures that must be strong to perform their functions; and all the parts that make up your body form a single complex solid structure.

1. Forms of Structures

    a. Frame: _____

            _____

    b. Shell: _____

            _____

    c. Solid: _____

            _____

2.

2 Centre of Gravity

A structure's centre of gravity is an important element to consider when designing a structure. We depend on our body's centre of gravity to do daily activities. In this unit, you will examine where the centre of gravity is in a structure, and how a structure's centre of gravity affects its stability.

After completing this unit, you will

- know the meaning of an object's centre of gravity.
- understand that a structure's centre of gravity affects its stability.

We are smart to use a balancing pole. It lowers our centre of gravity to make us more stable.

Vocabulary

centre of gravity: the point of an object where all the mass seems to be concentrated

stable: unlikely to move; firmly in place

block towers:

stable

not stable

When you were a baby, you might have played with tumbler toys. Tumbler toys are shaped like clowns or animals from the waist up and shaped like a hemisphere from the waist down. The rounded bottom half of a tumbler toy is weighted, while the top half is hollow, making the toy very bottom-heavy. No matter how hard a child pushes it, a tumbler toy is always able to right itself. Do you know how a tumbler toy's weight and shape allow it to always spring back to an upright position?

A. Fill in the blanks with the given words.

Centre of Gravity   **irregularly   mass   stable   regularly   centre   balance   changes**

The 1._____ of gravity is the point on a body or object where all the 2._____ seems to be concentrated. In a 3._____ shaped object, like a cube or ball, that point is the geometric centre. In 4._____ shaped objects, it is not as easy to find. In objects

We both are stable!

base

that shift or move, like our bodies, the centre of gravity 5._____ with each new position.

An object is 6._____ only if its centre of gravity is directly above its base or point of 7._____ .

B. Mark the centre of gravity (X) for each shape.

C. Circle the correct words. Then mark the centre of gravity for each object and colour the more stable object in each pair.

1. A structure's stability depends largely on where its **mass / colour** is concentrated. The **higher from / lower to** the ground a structure's mass is centred, the more stable it is. In other words, a **low / high** centre of gravity increases a structure's stability.

2.

3.

4.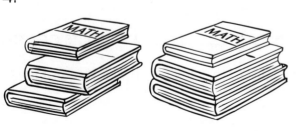

5.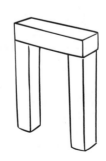

D. Look at the cargo ships. Then answer the questions.

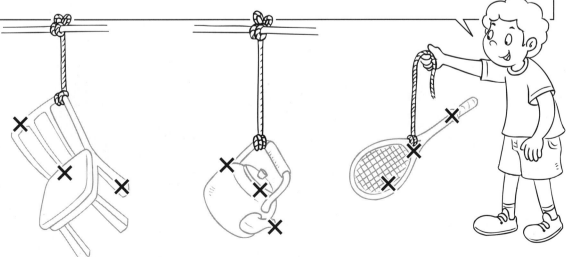

A

B

1. Which cargo ship is more stable? Explain.

    _____

    _____

2. In which cargo ship is the load more safely packed? Explain.

    _____

    _____

E. Circle the correct words. Then circle the point that is closest to the centre of gravity of each object.

The centre of gravity of an object is its **balance / middle** point. When an object is suspended, the centre of gravity will be directly **above / below** the suspension point.

F. Read the passage. Then answer the questions.

A Changing Centre of Gravity:
the Leaning Tower of Pisa

The Leaning Tower of Pisa is a very famous and much-visited bell tower in Italy. It is famous precisely because of its seemingly gravity-defying lean. While it may not look so, the tower is actually stable because its centre of gravity remains above its base.

When the tower was completed in 1350, it was already leaning well over 1 metre from the vertical. This inclination was the result of a poorly designed and shallow foundation set atop very soft, unstable ground. Over the years, the tower leaned more and more. By the early 1990s, it was leaning more than 5 metres from the vertical, and its centre of gravity was dangerously close to no longer being above its base: the tower was close to toppling. It was declared unsafe, and tourists were no longer allowed to climb the tower's stairs. Between 1991 and 2001, engineers from around the world worked to reduce its lean so that it would be stable and safe again. They dug out some dirt from beneath the higher end of the tower's foundation, piled lead weights at that end, and attached steel cables from the tower to the ground. These measures reduced the tower's lean by 45 centimetres. Now the tower is once again considered stable and safe to climb.

1. Record the distance shifted from the vertical of the Leaning Tower in the different years.

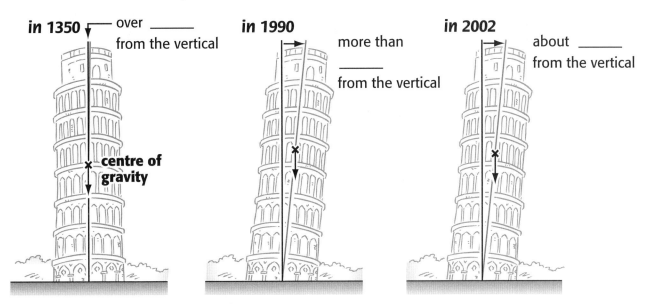

in 1350 — over _____ from the vertical

in 1990 — more than _____ from the vertical

in 2002 — about _____ from the vertical

centre of gravity

2. Where should the centre of gravity be for a building to remain stable?

_____

_____

3. Draw an **X** where you think the centre of gravity of each building is. Then check the stable buildings.

A   B   C   D   E

3 Forces and Structures

Forces push and pull on structures, sometimes to the point of destruction. Forces from inside and outside may cause structures to crush, bend, twist, or stretch. They do it with different amounts of intensity and from different directions. In this unit, you will examine internal and external forces that act on structures.

After completing this unit, you will

- understand how magnitude, direction, and point of application describe forces applied to a structure.
- understand the difference between internal and external forces that act on a structure.

This is a hurricane of great magnitude. Its force has already damaged many buildings.

vocabulary

force: a push or pull that causes movement or a change in shape

magnitude: size

external force: **rain**

internal force: **compression**

Extension

Many of the forces acting on structures come from nature, but these natural forces do not have to be hurricanes, tornadoes, or earthquakes; wind, rain, and snow act on structures, too, and can cause damage. The force of rain is strong enough to break down rock into soil. Mangled umbrellas are often the result of strong winds. Snow accumulating on a roof can become heavy enough to cause the roof to collapse.

Can you think of times when you have seen wind, rain, or snow cause damage to structures?

Record your observations.
Damages caused by...

Wind: _____

Rain: _____

Snow: _____

A. Fill in the blanks with the words that describe the pictures. Then match the pictures with the correct descriptions.

Internal and external forces act together to cause _____ on a structure, leading to the weakening of one or more of its parts.

When a structure's parts are weakened, it is called structural _____ .

Over a period of time, or when suddenly under extreme stress, this fatigue can cause structural _____ .

failure

stress

fatigue

B. Fill in the blanks to identify the external and internal forces on structures.

External Forces* on Structures
*pushing or pulling forces that act on structures

| an earthquake | still water |
| rain | gravity | wind |

1. _____ can crack the walls of many buildings.

2. _____ pushes against the glass of an aquarium.

3. _____ can be so strong that it knocks over trees.

4. _____ pushes on a boulder, smoothing its rough edges.

5. _____ causes a building to push on the ground it is built on.

Internal Forces on Structures

shear   compression   tension   torsion

6. A _____ force occurs when a load pushes on a structure. A building must have the compressive strength to carry the load of its occupants and their things, as well as the load of its own weight.

7. A pull is called a _____ force. The rope in a swing must have the tensile strength to withstand the pull of a child's weight.

8. A _____ force occurs when different parts of a structure are pressed in opposite directions. Using scissors to cut a sheet of paper is an example of this force.

9. A _____ force is the twisting of an object in opposite directions. A wet towel must have the torsion strength to withstand being wrung out.

C. Complete the descriptions. Then describe how the forces are different in each pair of pictures.

| point of application | magnitude | direction |

The amount of force on an object depends on the force's...

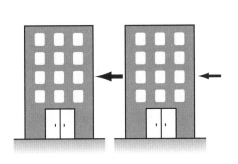 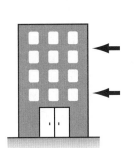 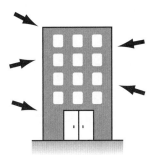

1. _____   2. _____   3. _____

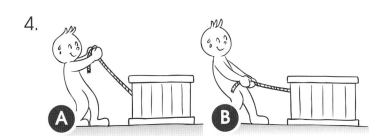

Amount of force on the box depends on: _____

A greater force is acting on box _____ .

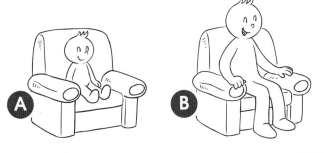

Amount of force on the couch depends on: _____

A greater force is acting on couch _____ .

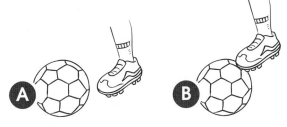

Amount of force on the ball depends on: _____

A greater force is acting on ball _____ .

D. Read the passage. Then answer the questions.

How to Measure an
Earthquake

Most scientists agree on two ways to measure an earthquake. The first way is to measure its magnitude, which is obtained by recording ground movement. The most commonly used scale to measure magnitude is the Richter Scale. An earthquake that is undetectable to a normal person has a reading below 2, at which point it is referred to as "minor", while one at a reading of 9, which is referred to as "great", can cause serious damage to areas several hundred kilometres away from its point of origin.

The second way is to measure an earthquake's intensity, which is not a mathematical measurement but a compilation of observations regarding the earthquake's effects on structures and people. Canada uses the Modified Mercalli Intensity (MMI) Scale, which has 12 levels of intensity, each with its own set of observations. At MMI I, the first level, an earthquake's effects are "instrumental", or barely perceptible. At MMI XII, the final level, they are "catastrophic" – there is total destruction.

While an earthquake only has one measurement of magnitude, its measurement of intensity changes depending on how close a person or structure is to the earthquake's centre. The 2010 earthquake in Haiti measured 7.0 on the Richter Scale. On the MMI Scale, it measured MMI IX ("ruinous") in the country's capital, Port-au-Prince. In Guantanamo, Cuba, 350 km away, it measured MMI III ("slight").

1. Name the two measures of an earthquake and describe what they represent and how they are obtained.

   a. _____ : _____

      _____

   b. _____ : _____

      _____

2. Complete the two scales used to measure earthquakes.

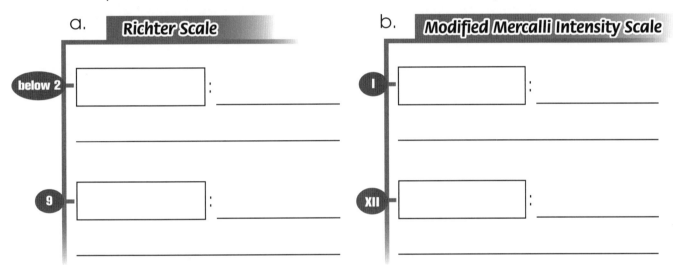

3. Write the measures of the 2010 Haiti earthquake. Then find one earthquake record on your own.

   a. 2010 Haiti Earthquake

       • magnitude (Richter Scale): _____

       • intensity (MMI Scale): _____ at _____

                              _____ at _____

   b. _____

       • magnitude (Richter Scale): _____

       • intensity (MMI Scale): _____ at _____

                              _____ at _____

Introduction

We are moving structures. We can walk, jump, run, dive, crouch, and bend over without toppling over or becoming unstable. This is because as our centre of gravity changes, we adjust our bodies to remain stable.

Hypothesis

When we bend over, we   do not need / need   to adjust our lower body to remain stable.

Steps

1. Have a partner (your friend, sibling, or parent) to help you with this experiment.

2. Stand with your back and heels up against the wall.

3. Have your partner place the small object about 30 cm in front of you on the floor.

4. Without bending your knees or moving your feet, try to bend over to pick up the object.

Materials

- *wall*
- *a small object (tennis ball, hockey puck, plastic cup, etc.)*

5. Step away from the wall and try to bend over at the hips to pick up the object.

6. Have your partner do steps 2 to 5.

7. Record your observations in the chart below.

✔/✘	Picked up object when	
	against the wall	away from the wall
Me		
My Partner:		

Result

1. Could you pick up the object

   • when your body was against the wall?   _____

   • when your body was away from the wall?   _____

2. What, if anything, was different between these two positions?

   _____

Conclusion

The hypothesis was: _____

   _____

My experiment _____ the hypothesis.
                                    supported/did not support

4 More about Structures

Symmetry is a common feature in the design of structures. We can compare symmetry in design to the symmetry of balanced forces on a structure. In this unit, you will examine the role of symmetry in structures. You will learn to use arrows to show balanced or unbalanced forces in a structure. You will also learn about ergonomics.

After completing this unit, you will

- understand that symmetry is important in the design of a structure.

- understand that we can use arrows to show the relative strength of opposing forces on a structure.

- understand what ergonomics is.

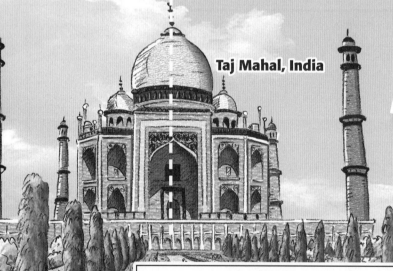

line of symmetry

Taj Mahal, India

Daddy, don't you think that this symmetrical building is beautiful?

v o c a b u l a r y

symmetry: being the same on both sides

ergonomics: designing structures to fit the user

asymmetrical: not symmetrical

snowflake: a symmetrical structure

imaginary line

Most living things are symmetrical. If you make an imaginary line from the head of a butterfly to the ground, one side basically looks like the other. What do you think about your own body? You can see that you are a symmetrical structure too. Symmetrical structures look good and they can be aesthetically pleasing to the eye. Can you list five natural symmetrical structures that are aesthetically pleasing to you?

A. Circle the correct words. Then check the symmetrical structures and draw one more example of a symmetrical structure.

Symmetry is the **similarity / sameness** of opposite sides: an imaginary line, called the line of symmetry, divides a structure into **two / three**, and each half is a **fun / mirror** image of the other half.

Symmetrical Structures

Ⓐ Ⓑ Ⓒ Ⓓ

B. Fill in the blanks to complete the paragraphs. Label the diagrams.

> tension   stability   uneven   base   compression   even   symmetrical

Stability in Symmetrical Structures

Symmetry improves the 1._____ of structures. If the centre of gravity of a structure is above the centre of its support 2._____ , it can resist external forces better than a structure that is not thus aligned. Building 3.____ is a more stable structure.

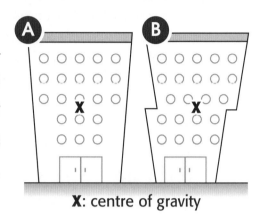

X: centre of gravity

A load on a structure works better if it is 4._____ , or evenly distributed on the structure. A dead load placed unevenly on a structure creates extra 5._____ and 6._____ that cause instability and possibly even a failure to support the load.

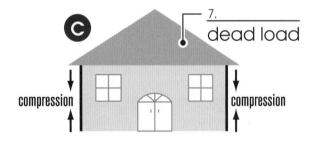
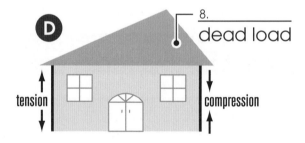

Building 9.____ is a more stable structure.

C. Draw to complete the symmetrical structures.

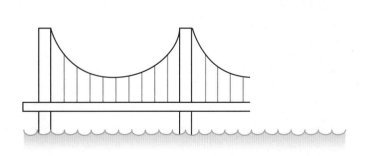
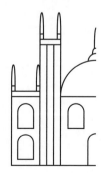

D. Fill in the blanks with the given words. Then draw the missing arrows in each picture.

Balanced and Unbalanced Forces

| balanced | greater | strength |

The thickness of an arrow representing a force indicates its

1._____ . When two arrows are the same size, the forces are

2._____ . When one arrow is thicker, it has a 3._____ force

than the one it is opposing.

4. *Scenario 1*

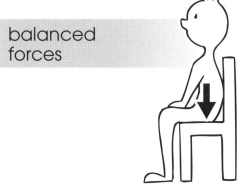

balanced forces

unbalanced forces

5. *Scenario 2*

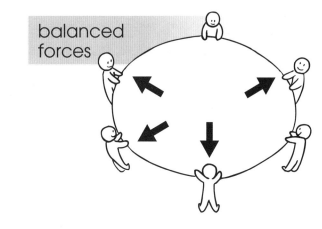

balanced forces

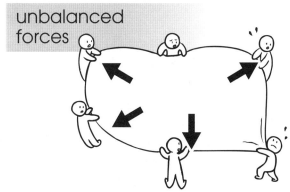

unbalanced forces

6. Why can balanced forces be referred to as symmetrical?

_____

7. What can happen to a structure if the forces are asymmetrical?

_____

E. Read the passage. Then answer the questions.

The goal of an ergonomically designed work station in an office setting is to ensure that a worker can maintain a comfortable and safe sitting position. To maintain a comfortable and safe sitting position, our feet must be flat on the floor or raised slightly on a footrest; our knees should be bent at a 90° angle, while our thighs are parallel to the floor; our shoulders should be relaxed with our elbows at a 90° angle; our lower arms should be parallel to the floor; our hips, back, and neck should form a straight line; and the distance between our eyes and a computer screen should be 45 to 60 centimetres. In order to achieve this position, an office chair

Ergonomics:
Making Structures Fit People

and desk must be carefully designed. An office chair's height from the seat to the floor and its backrest and armrest positions should be adjustable. The chair's backrest should be designed to relieve pressure from the lower back, and many are designed with a bump where the lower back rests for this purpose. The desk should be adjustable to provide the correct elbow and knee angle, foot position, and computer viewing distance.

1. Check the workstation that is ergonomically designed. Then describe the highlighted parts in the design.

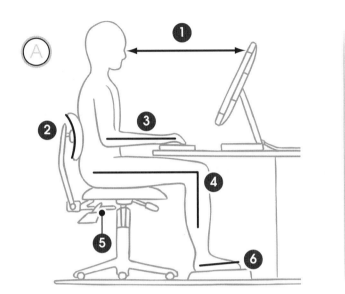 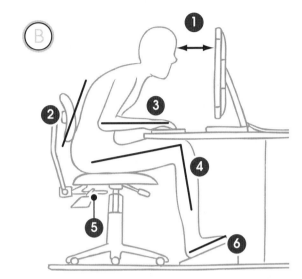

Descriptions of the highlighted parts:

1 _____

2 _____

3 _____

4 _____

5 _____

6 _____

2. Check the things that have an ergonomical design.

5 Loads and Structural Failure

A broken or collapsed structure cannot fulfill its function. For some structures, this can be costly and even dangerous. To build sturdy structures, it is necessary to know what causes failure. In this unit, you will examine the causes of structural failure, and look at the consequences of some structural failures.

After completing this unit, you will

- understand that many factors can cause a structure to fail.

- understand that considering a structure's purpose before building helps prevent structural failure.

> *Mom, the wind is so strong. It causes the structural failure of our umbrella.*

Vocabulary

dead load: the weight or forces that are part of a structure

live load: the variable weight of forces acting on a structure

structural failure: a collapsed or broken structure

live load: girl

dead load: tires

A famous failure! A sensational success! A structure can become one or the other, depending on how it was built. Though it is still standing, the Leaning Tower of Pisa is a famous failure. Amazingly, the ancient Egyptian pyramids are still standing despite their age. They are a sensational success.

Go for a walk in your neighbourhood and look at structures like fences, sidewalks, spiderwebs, and trees. Try to figure out what makes them successful, or what has caused them to fail.

Leaning Tower of Pisa

The Pyramids of Giza

A. Fill in the blanks with the given words.

Live Loads and Dead Loads

roof   failure   force   greater   load
wind   snow   gravity   collapse

All structures are made to withstand some level of 1._____ .
Force acting on a structure is called a 2._____ . A load may be one of two types: a dead load or a live load. A dead load acts on a structure all the time. 3._____ is an example of a dead load. For a house, another dead load is the weight of the 4._____ . Examples of live loads are the weight of 5._____ on a roof, the people that gather on a balcony, or the 6._____ that occasionally blows against a building. When any load is 7._____ than a structure can bear, it puts stress on the structure, which can lead to breakage or 8._____ . This is structural 9._____ .

B. Write the factor that can cause structural failure and complete the description for each situation.

Factors that Can Cause Structural Failure

poor design poor workmanship oversized loads foundation failure unsuitable materials	sinking high snow rusting poorly

1. Factor: _____

The building has a _____ centre of gravity.

2. Factor: _____

The iron is _____ in the salty air.

3. Factor: _____

Heavy _____ accumulates on the roof.

4. Factor: _____

The house is _____ into the ground.

5. Factor: _____

The frame has _____ fitted beams.

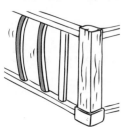

C. What could be done to improve the design of the structures shown on the previous page so that they do not fail? Write the suggestions on the lines.

1 The redesigned building should have a _____ base. This can _____ the

           bigger/smaller   lower/raise

centre of gravity.

2 _____

    _____

3 _____

    _____

4 _____

    _____

5 _____

    _____

D. Suggest what could be changed in each picture to improve the design so that there is less chance of structural failure.

1.

2. **cardboard**

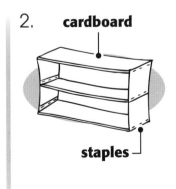

staples

E. Read the passage. Then answer the questions.

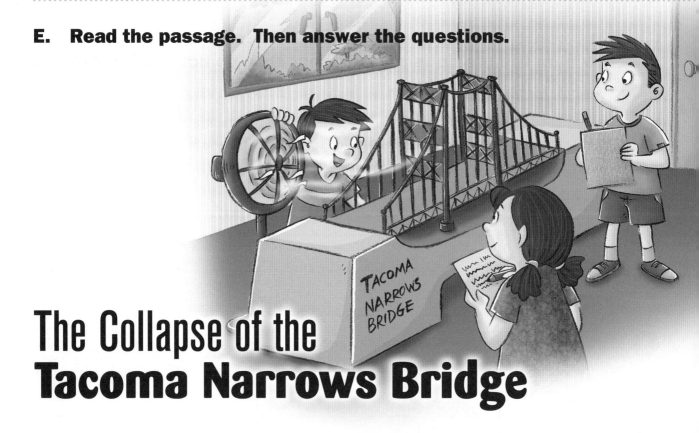

The Collapse of the Tacoma Narrows Bridge

The original Tacoma Narrows Bridge was a suspension bridge that spanned the Tacoma Narrows in Washington, U.S.A. It opened on July 1, 1940; on November 7 of the same year, the bridge collapsed.

Engineers still disagree about what exactly caused the collapse of the Tacoma Narrows Bridge. They do agree on some points though: the bridge's design made the bridge too flexible, and it did not take into account the force of wind. The bridge was built to be slender and very long, with relatively thin steel girders supporting the deck. The use of these thin girders resulted in a very flexible bridge that lacked the stiffness required to resist winds, so it rolled vertically even in light winds. On the day of the collapse, this vertical roll became a twisting movement after one of the bridge's cables slipped and became uneven: the bridge was not strong enough to withstand this torsion force. The cables snapped, and the bridge fell into Puget Sound.

Though considered a catastrophe, the collapse was a valuable learning experience: engineers fixed the bridge by adding reinforced trusses along the girder. Before the collapse, engineers believed that traffic was the main live load to be considered when designing a bridge; wind was only a minor consideration. Today, bridge designs undergo extensive tests involving wind tunnels and are studied using computer programs that simulate wind before the bridges are built.

1. Complete the picture of a typical suspension bridge and name the components.

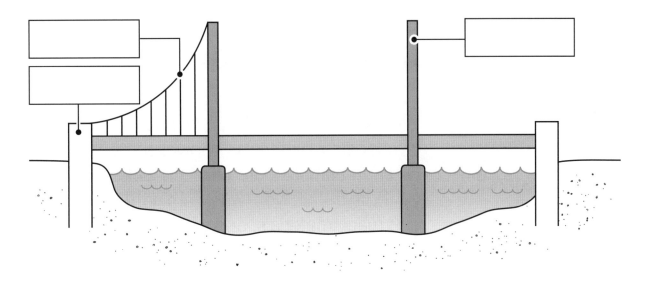

2. What was the main structural factor that caused the collapse of the Tacoma Narrows Bridge?

_____

_____

_____

3. What triggered the collapse of the Tacoma Narrows Bridge? What force was in action before the bridge fell into Puget Sound?

_____

_____

_____

4. Check the repaired Tacoma Narrows Bridge.

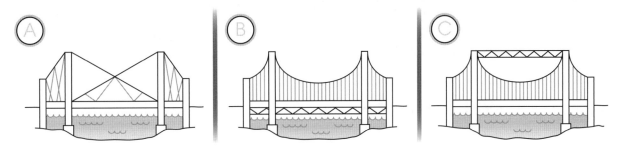

6 Materials and Structures

All structures are made from at least one material. Ideally, a structure's function is the main factor in choosing materials. However, cost, availability, and aesthetics are often considerations as well. In this unit, you will examine the properties of many materials, and why different materials are chosen for different structures.

After completing this unit, you will

- understand that materials are chosen for their properties.
- understand that other factors may dictate the material chosen for a structure.

Mom, this backpack is made from different materials and it is light and waterproof. It is a good idea to use it for outdoor activities.

nylon fabric: waterproofed with a heavy wax coating

50% cotton 50% nylon

composite material

Vocabulary

aesthetic: pleasing appearance

strength: the ability to withstand force

composite material: a material made from two or more materials

Extension

Some materials are a combination of different materials. Materials are mixed so that they can have the advantageous properties of all the materials used. However, sometimes, instead of mixing materials to make a better material, materials are mixed mainly to make a product less expensive to produce.

fibreglass: glass + plastic
properties: strong, lightweight, durable, waterproof

particle board: wood particles + resin
properties: not as strong as wood, inexpensive

Which of these two composite materials has the advantages of the properties of its constituent materials?

A. Choose the thing that has a greater strength in each pair and fill in the blanks.

Internal Forces

torsion   compression   shear   tension

A Torsion Strength

_____ can withstand a greater

_____ .

B Shear Strength

_____ can withstand a greater

_____ .

C Tensile Strength

_____ can withstand a greater

_____ .

D Compressive Strength

_____ can withstand a greater

_____ .

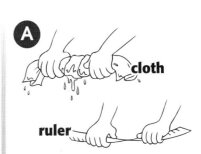

cloth

ruler

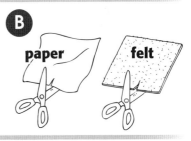

paper   felt

rope

spaghetti

wood

jelly

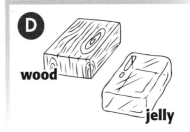

B. **Write two properties of materials that would be considered when making each structure. Then suggest the materials to be used and explain your choice.**

Properties of Materials

elasticity   strength   hardness   weight
flexibility   warmth   water resistance
durability   lustre   transparency

Materials

steel   aluminum   cotton
rubber   leather   vinyl
plastic   wool   concrete

1. Properties of materials: _____ and _____

    Materials to be used: _____ and _____

    Explain: _____

    _____

    winter boots

2. Properties of materials: _____ and _____

    Materials to be used: _____ and _____

    Explain: _____

    _____

    laptop

3. Properties of materials: _____ and _____

    Materials to be used: _____ and _____

    Explain: _____

    _____

    plastic wrap

4. Properties of materials: _____ and _____

    Materials to be used: _____ and _____

    Explain: _____

    _____

    garden fountain

C. Write the factor to consider when choosing a material in each situation. Then answer the questions.

Factors

aesthetic   cost   availability

5. Do the above factors relate to a material's strength or durability?

   _____

6. Write about a situation where one of these factors was a more important consideration than a material's strength or durability.

   _____

   _____

D. Read the passage. Then answer the questions.

Consider This When Choosing Materials:
the Environment

When choosing materials for structures, one consideration is becoming increasingly important to many designers, builders, and consumers: a material's environmental impact.

One example of this consideration is the choice of materials for shopping bags. Worldwide, the plastic shopping bag is consumers' preferred way of holding goods. A conservative estimate places the number of plastic bags used each year at 500 billion. It is easy to see why plastic bags are so widely used: they are strong, inexpensive, and plentiful. However, only a small percentage of these bags are recycled, and the bags that end up in landfills can take hundreds of years to break down. Many bags end up as litter, suffocating wildlife, polluting water, and releasing toxic materials. Plastic shopping bags are bad for the environment.

In response, many consumers have started using reusable shopping bags. These bags can be made from long-lasting plastic or cloth. They are stronger and more aesthetically pleasing than plastic bags, and they ensure that fewer plastic bags end up in landfills or as litter. These "green" shopping bags are, however, more expensive than plastic bags. The same is true for many structures made from environmentally friendly materials: one must weigh the higher initial financial cost with the lower long-term environmental cost when choosing materials.

1. Colour each bar to show the strength of a plastic bag. Then give three properties of a plastic bag that make it widely used.

Strength of a Plastic Bag

	weak	great
Torsion		
Shear		
Tension		
Compression		

Properties of a Plastic Bag

_____

_____

_____

2. What effects do plastic bags have on the environment?

_____

_____

_____

3. What alternatives to plastic bags do environmentalists recommend? What properties does the alternative material have? Check the circles and explain your choice.

An alternative to the plastic bag: _____

Properties of the Alternative Material:

(A) durable   (B) heavy   (C) biodegradable

(D) transparent   (E) washable   (F) high viscosity

(G) foldable   (H) lightweight   (I) reusable

Explain:

_____

_____

Experiment

Introduction

Have you ever broken a shoelace? A broken shoelace is an example of a material that has been pulled beyond its tensile strength. Different materials can handle different amounts of tension, which means they differ in their tensile strength. Do you know which materials have more tensile strength than others?

Hypothesis

Put the four materials in order according to their tensile strength: ribbon, twine, thread, paper clip.

From strongest to weakest, the materials are _____ , _____ , _____ , and _____ .

Materials

- *a basket with handle*
- *2 chairs*
- *a broom*
- *books for weight*
- *a 40-cm chain of paper clips*
- *40-cm pieces of ribbon, twine, thread*

Steps

1. Place the broom across the backs of two chairs that are set no more than a metre apart.

2. Tie one end of the ribbon around the broom and the other end around the basket's handle.

3. Add books to the basket, one at a time, until the ribbon breaks.

4. Repeat with the twine, thread, and paper clip chains. Be sure to add the books in the same order for each material tested.

Result

Record the number of books each material held before it broke:

ribbon: _____ books   twine: _____

thread: _____   paper clips: _____

Were you surprised at which material had

- the greatest tensile strength? _____

- the lowest tensile strength?   _____

Go a step further!

Can a material be made stronger by doubling it? Try using two or more pieces of each material at the same time.

Conclusion

The hypothesis was: _____

_____

My experiment _____ the hypothesis.
                    supported/did not support

Try to complete this review in **30 minutes**.

30 minutes

This review consists of five sections, from A to E. The marks for each question are shown in parentheses. The circle at the bottom right corner is for the marks you get in each section. An overall record is on the last page of the review.

A. Write T for true and F for false.

1. Weightlifting is an example of compression force. **(2)**   _____

2. All symmetrical structures are stable. **(2)**   _____

3. Gravity is an example of a live load. **(2)**   _____

4. The height of a structure is one of the factors that affect the centre of gravity of the structure. **(2)**   _____

5. Rain is an external force that acts on a structure. **(2)**

   _____

6. The structure is asymmetrical, so it must be unstable. **(2)**

   _____

12

B. Do the matching.

1.  (3)

2. 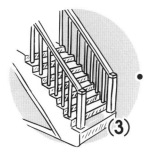 (3)

3.  (3)

4.  (3)

5.  (3)

6. 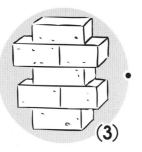 (3)

- an example of a shell

- a structural failure

- a dead load

- has high tensile strength

- apply a shear force to work

- having a wider base will improve its stability

C. **See how Karen made her pencil holder out of popsicle sticks, cardboard, and aluminum foil. Then answer the questions.**

1. Identify the form and function of popsicle sticks and aluminum foil in the pencil holder.

    Popsicle Sticks

    form: _____ **(2)**

    function: _____

    _____ **(3)**

    Aluminum Foil

    form: _____ **(2)**

    function: _____

    _____ **(3)**

2. Check what can be done to make the pencil holder more stable. Explain your choice. **(6)**

    (A) Use longer popsicle sticks.

    (B) Use fewer sticks and less foil.

    (C) Thicken the base by layering it with pieces of cardboard.

    Explain: _____

    _____

3. If Karen uses plastic wrap instead of aluminum foil, do you think it will increase the stability of her pencil holder? Explain. **(4)**

    _____

    _____

Karen's Pencil Holder

1 Glue the sticks on the foil. Then put another piece of foil on top.

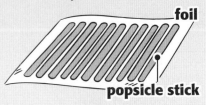

foil

popsicle stick

2 Roll up the foil and put the cardboard at one end of the cylinder. Then glue to hold the cardboard in place.

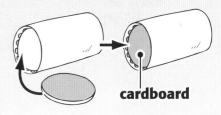

cardboard

3 Press the foil along the edge.

Done!

20

D. Jason has tested the stability of the three stools that he built by putting books on them. Answer the questions.

A — wooden boards and screws

B — wooden boards and screws

C — foam boards and glue

1. Draw lines to match the number of books that each stool can support. Then explain your guess. **(12)**

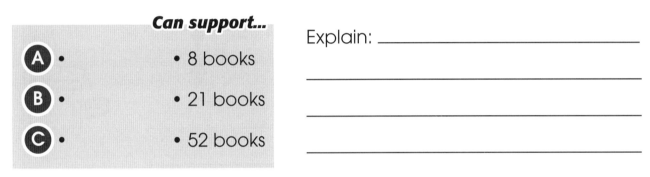

Can support...

A •

B •

C •

• 8 books

• 21 books

• 52 books

Explain: _____

_____

_____

_____

2. If Jason wants to adjust the height of stool Ⓐ so as to make it more stable, what should he do? Explain your idea. **(4)**

_____

_____

3. Write the definitions of live load and dead load. Then identify the live load and the dead load in the picture.

(3)

live load: _____

(3)

dead load: _____

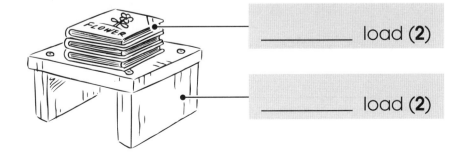

_____ load **(2)**

_____ load **(2)**

26

E. Check the correct answer(s) for each question. Then explain your choice.

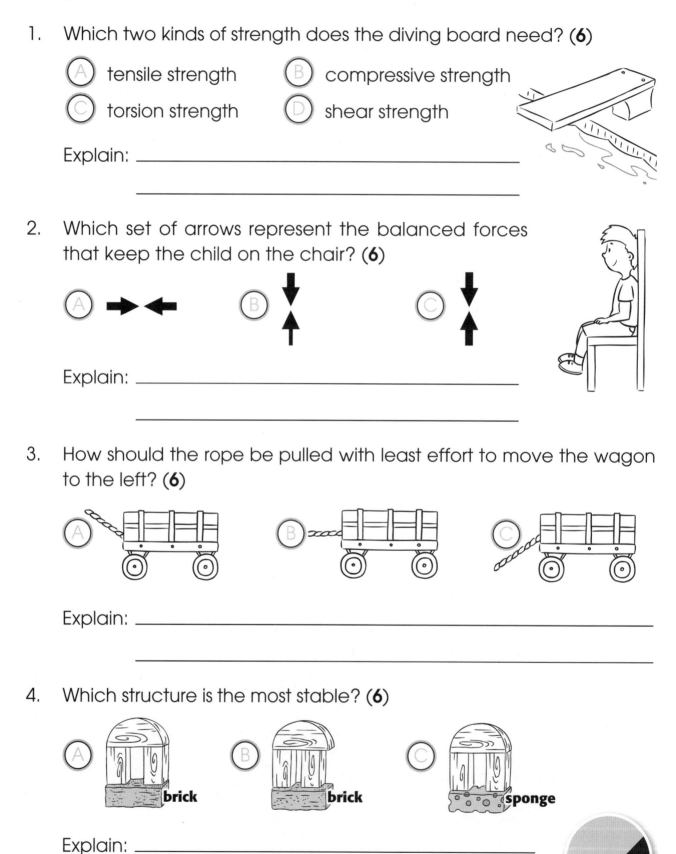

1. Which two kinds of strength does the diving board need? **(6)**

   Ⓐ tensile strength   Ⓑ compressive strength

   Ⓒ torsion strength   Ⓓ shear strength

   Explain: _____

   _____

2. Which set of arrows represent the balanced forces that keep the child on the chair? **(6)**

   Ⓐ →←   Ⓑ ↓↑   Ⓒ ↓↑

   Explain: _____

   _____

3. How should the rope be pulled with least effort to move the wagon to the left? **(6)**

   Ⓐ   Ⓑ   Ⓒ

   Explain: _____

   _____

4. Which structure is the most stable? **(6)**

   Ⓐ brick   Ⓑ brick   Ⓒ sponge

   Explain: _____

   _____

24

My Record

Section A	12
Section B	18
Section C	20
Section D	26
Section E	24

Total

100

 **80-100**

Great work! You really understand your science stuff! Research your favourite science topics at the library or on the Internet to find out more about the topics related to this section. Keep challenging yourself to learn more!

 **60-79**

Good work! You understand some basic concepts, but try reading through the units again to see whether you can master the material! Go over the questions that you had trouble with to make sure you know the correct answers.

 **below 60**

You can do much better! Try reading over the units again. Ask your parents or teachers any questions you might have. Once you feel confident that you know the material, try the review again. Science is exciting, so don't give up!

The Packaging Engineer

Robert Gair

You must have seen cartons, which are made of cardboard and yet are strong and sturdy enough to hold heavy objects. Corrugated paper was invented in England in the 1850s. At first it was used as a liner for tall hats. Later Albert Jones of New York City used corrugated board to wrap bottles and glass lantern chimneys so that they would not be damaged or broken in transit. The first machine for producing large quantities of corrugated board was built in 1874 by G. Smyth, and in the same year Oliver Long improved upon Jones' design by inventing corrugated board with liner sheets on both sides. This was corrugated board as we know it today.

Then in 1890 Robert Gair, a printer and paper-bag maker in Brooklyn, invented the pre-cut paperboard box. The flat pieces manufactured in bulk could be folded into boxes. Gair's invention actually came about as a result of an accident. One day, while he was printing an order of seed bags, a metal ruler used for creasing bags shifted in position and cut them. Gair discovered that by cutting and creasing in one operation, he could make prefabricated paperboard boxes!

Jones, Smyth, Long, and Gair each improved on the use of corrugated board for packaging and can all be considered to be the first packaging engineers.

Cool Science Facts

1 How does a whistle work?

2 We can see ourselves in a mirror, but do you know what is inside a mirror?

Don't Step on GRASS

3 Why do the bottoms of aerosol cans always curve inward?

4 Why do bees build honeycombs in hexagons and not in other shapes?

All honeycombs are in the shape of hexagon.

Find the answers on the next page.

Cool Science Facts

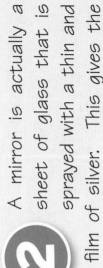

1

When you blow into a whistle, the air separates into two streams — one goes straight and one curls around. Since both air streams rush out of the whistle through the same air slot, it causes an unstable condition – turbulence. This turbulence creates a strong air vibration which makes sound. Therefore, if you block the slot of the whistle while your blow, no sound will be made.

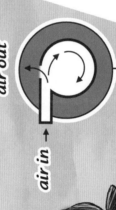

air out
air in

2

A mirror is actually a sheet of glass that is sprayed with a thin and even film of silver. This gives the mirror a highly reflective surface. Then a thin coat of copper is sprayed onto the silver to protect it from wearing out and make the mirror more durable. This is why a mirror is smooth and reflective on the front and dull at the back.

3

Since all aerosol cans contain pressurized gas, if the bottom of a can were flat, the gas inside it might push the bottom outward. In contrast, a curved bottom works like a dome by distributing the force to the circular edge of the can. Moreover, the curved shape makes it easier to use up the product. If it were a flat bottom, you would have to tilt the can to collect the product. With a curved bottom, the last bit of product is collected around the edge of the can, making it easier to empty the product.

4

If the bees make the honeycomb in another shape, for example pentagon, there will be areas left unused between the cells; in that way, they will have to waste wax to patch these gaps. Although tiling squares or triangles will leave no gaps, hexagon is the shape that gives the greatest circumference with the same amount of wax. In other words, bees can store the greatest amount of honey in hexagonal cells while using the least amount of wax.

Section **3**

Understanding
Matter and
Energy

Scan this QR code or go to Download Centre at
www.popularbook.ca for some fun scientific
explorations!

A Coin Jump

Discover that heated air expands and can cause
movements.

A Milk Colour Explosion

Explore what soap does to mixtures.

1 The Particle Theory of Matter

Everything in the world – matter – is made up of particles. Understanding how particles work can help you understand how substances form and change. In this unit, you will examine matter, particles, and how particles behave in the different states of matter.

After completing this unit, you will

- understand that matter is made up of particles.
- understand that particles behave differently, depending on what state they are in.
- know the particle theory of matter.

Jimmy, look at this model of a solid sugar cube. It shows the particles packed closely together.

a model of a sugar cube

Particles

Vocabulary

matter: physical substance; has mass and takes up space

particle: one of the small pieces that make up matter

state: refers to the solid, liquid, or gas state of matter

liquid ⎯ gas ⎯ solid

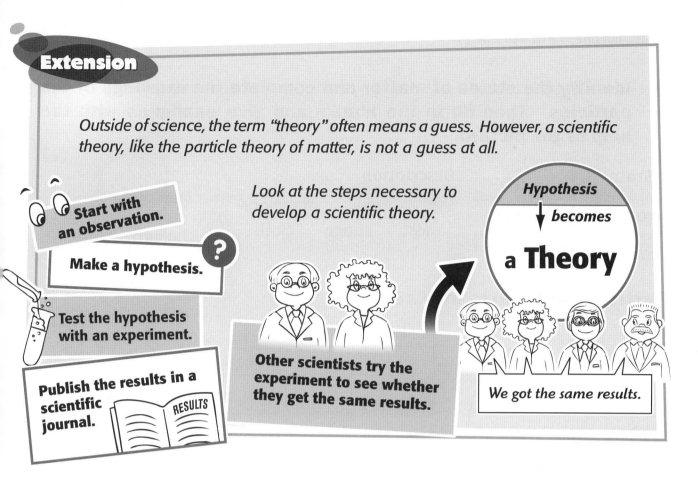

Outside of science, the term "theory" often means a guess. However, a scientific theory, like the particle theory of matter, is not a guess at all.

Start with an observation.

Make a hypothesis.

Test the hypothesis with an experiment.

Publish the results in a scientific journal.

RESULTS

Look at the steps necessary to develop a scientific theory.

Other scientists try the experiment to see whether they get the same results.

Hypothesis

becomes

a Theory

We got the same results.

A. Fill in the blanks to complete the sentences.

Particle Theory of Matter

the same
weak
particles
heat
space
moving
forces

1. Matter is made up of _____ .

2. Particles are always _____ .

3. There is _____ between particles.

4. _____ causes particles to move faster.

5. All particles in a substance are _____ .

6. 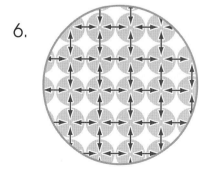 Attractive _____ hold particles together. Particles in solids have strong attractive forces and particles in gases have very _____ attractive forces.

B. Identify the states of matter and complete the drawings of the particles. Then fill in the blanks and give examples with the help of the picture.

State			Description		
gas	solid	liquid	slip	barely	directions
			most	space	close

helium

water — bottle

Particles and States of Matter

1.

Particles are very _____ together and can _____ move.

Examples: _____ and _____
my example

2.

Particles have more _____ between them than they do in solids and can _____ past each other.

Examples: _____ and _____
my example

3.

Particles have the _____ space between them and can move in all _____ .

Examples: _____ and _____
my example

C. Read the paragraph. Use the words in bold to complete the diagram and write whether heat is "added" or "taken away". Then draw the particles in each state and complete what the boy says.

*Water is unique because we can see its three states, but what causes a change in state? It is heat! When you remove an ice cube from the freezer, heat is added to the ice. The heat causes the ice particles to move faster and slip past each other, turning the ice into a liquid in a process called **melting**. Now you have water. If you boil the water in a pot, heat causes the particles to move so fast that some particles escape from the liquid as steam in a process called **evaporation**. Conversely, if heat is taken away from steam, it turns into liquid in a process called **condensation**. Liquid turns to ice when heat is taken away, too, and this is called **freezing**.*

1.

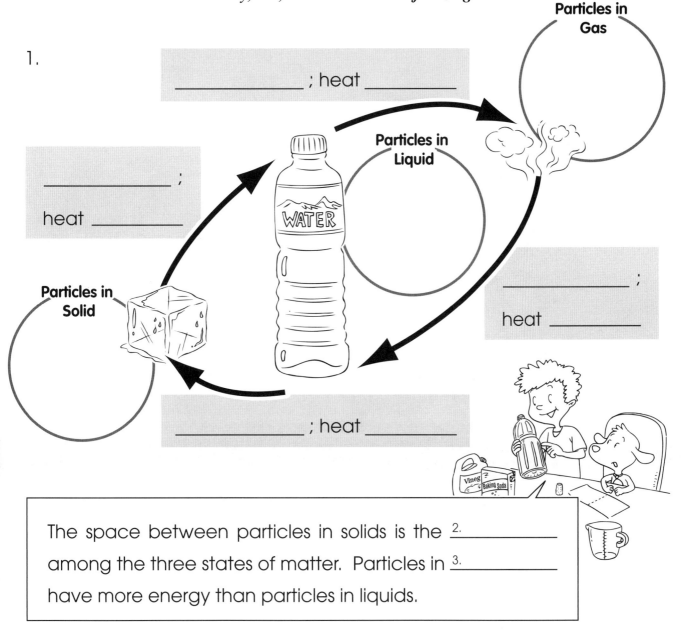

Particles in Gas

_____ ; heat _____

Particles in Liquid

_____ ;

heat _____

Particles in Solid

_____ ;

heat _____

_____ ; heat _____

The space between particles in solids is the ²._____ among the three states of matter. Particles in ³._____ have more energy than particles in liquids.

2 Pure Substances and Mixtures

A pure substance is made up of only one type of particle. While there are a limited number of pure substances in the world, the number of mixtures is endless. In this unit, you will examine the difference between pure substances and mixtures.

After completing this unit, you will

- understand that the particle theory of matter can explain the difference between a pure substance and a mixture.

- understand how pure substances are different from mixtures.

Can I have a bowl of mixture?

Fruit salad is a mixture. Do you mean you want a bowl of fruit salad?

Vocabulary

pure substance: matter with only one type of particle

mixture: matter with two or more types of particles

a pure substance
Refined Sugar

Most substances we see in our daily lives are mixtures. Pure substances are rarely found in nature. Water, a common substance in the world, exists in various types.

Look for different kinds of water in stores. Check their labels to see what is in them and record their contents.

Mineral/Spring water:
water that contains minerals

Iceberg water:
pure water

A. Determine whether each substance is a "pure substance" or a "mixture".

1.

a bowl of fruit salad:

_____

juice in watermelons:

_____

sugar in grapes:

_____

2.

steel rod

carbon: _____

iron: _____

steel: _____

○ : iron
/ : carbon

3. **Composition of Air**

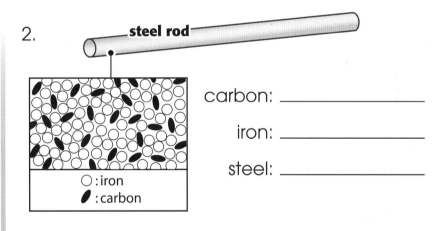

nitrogen: _____

oxygen: _____

air: _____

B. **Read the paragraph. Then complete the diagram with the words in bold and the pictures.**

*All **matter** is either a **pure substance**, which contains one type of particle, or a **mixture**, which contains more than one type of particle. A mixture can be a **solution**, where the parts join together, or it can be a **mechanical mixture**, where we can see the different parts.*

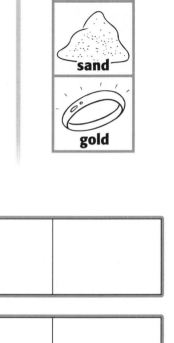

Examples

sea water

sand

gold

All about

Matter

the world

air

C. **Colour the particles to match the descriptions.**

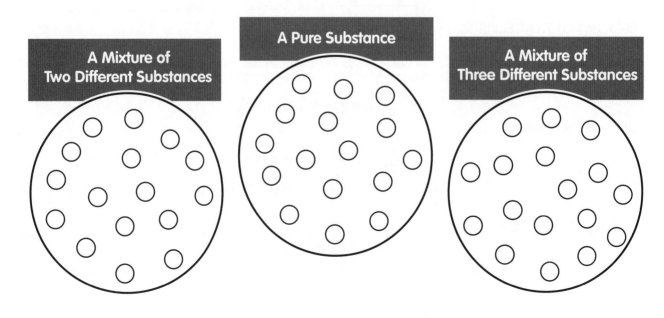

A Mixture of
Two Different Substances

A Pure Substance

A Mixture of
Three Different Substances

D. Read the paragraphs. Then answer the questions.

One of the most valued pure substances in our time – and perhaps in the history of the world – is gold. Since gold is lustrous and beautiful, it has been used for centuries to make coins, ornaments, and artwork. As the most malleable metal known and an excellent conductor of electricity, gold is also widely used in industry. Additionally, it is not subject to the corrosive effects of air, water, and most chemicals, which means that it does not react with them; therefore, gold objects that were beautiful, shiny, and valuable thousands of years ago are still so today.

Most other pure substances, however, do become corroded. Copper roofing reacts with air to develop a green coating, as seen on the Parliament Buildings in Ottawa; and products made from the metal iron, such as ships and cars, eventually become unusable because iron rusts when it reacts with air and water.

This gold mask was sealed in the tomb of an Egyptian king more than 3000 years ago.

1. **About Gold:**

    * _____ substance
    * malleability: **high / low**
    * reactivity with air, water, and most chemicals: **high / low / no**

    * lustre: **high / low**
    * conductivity: **high / low**

2. Write two more pure substances mentioned in the paragraphs and describe their properties and uses. Then write an example of your own.

a. _____	b. _____	c. _____
pure substance	pure substance	pure substance
_____	_____	_____
_____	_____	_____
_____	_____	_____
_____	_____	_____

3 Solutions and Mechanical Mixtures

All mixtures are made up of more than one pure substance, but they do not all mix in the same way. Some become solutions and others are mechanical mixtures. In this unit, you will identify everyday mixtures as solutions or mechanical mixtures.

Mom, let me show you what a mechanical mixture is.

After completing this unit, you will

- know which substances are solutions and which are mechanical mixtures.
- understand that solutions are homogeneous mixtures and mechanical mixtures are heterogeneous.

Vocabulary

homogeneous: all parts are the same throughout

heterogeneous: parts are different and can be separated

solution: homogeneous mixture of substances

mechanical mixture: heterogeneous mixture of substances

alloy: a solution of two or more pure substances, at least one of which is metallic

pizza: a heterogeneous mixture

Lots of things around us are mixtures, like the air we breathe or the ink that we use for writing. As we know, air is a mixture of nitrogen, oxygen, carbon dioxide, and other gases. What about black ink? What other coloured inks are mixed to make black ink? Try the little experiment described below to find the answer.

Draw a black spot in the centre of a dry coffee filter with a marker. Then put a few drops of water on the spot.

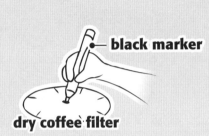

black marker — water

dry coffee filter

In a few minutes, you will see rings of colour that go out from the centre of the filter to the edge. You can see that black ink is a mixture of red, blue, and yellow inks.

A. Fill in the blanks to complete the paragraph. Then check the correct circles.

| heterogeneous | different | mechanical mixture | properties |

A mixture can be either a 1._____ or a solution. In a mechanical mixture, each substance keeps its own 2._____ . Usually the different substances can be identified within the mixture. When you make chicken fried rice, you can see the 3._____ parts of the mixture. This is a sign that the mixture is 4._____ .

Examples of
Mechanical Mixtures

A

sweetened
iced tea

B

cereal and milk

C

sand and
rocks

D

milk

B. Fill in the blanks with the correct words. Then complete the diagram and put the mixtures into the correct categories.

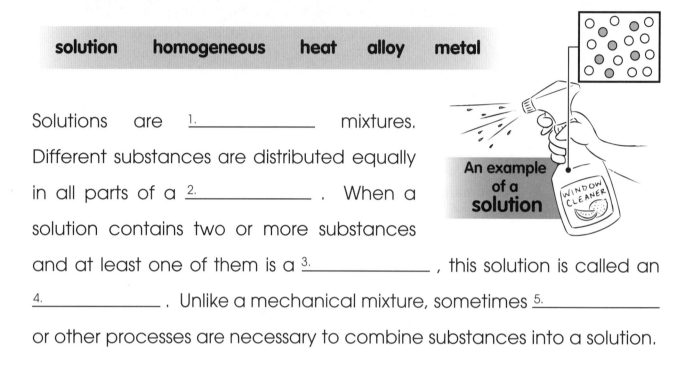

solution   homogeneous   heat   alloy   metal

Solutions are 1._____ mixtures. Different substances are distributed equally in all parts of a 2._____ . When a solution contains two or more substances and at least one of them is a 3._____ , this solution is called an 4._____ . Unlike a mechanical mixture, sometimes 5._____ or other processes are necessary to combine substances into a solution.

An example of a **solution**

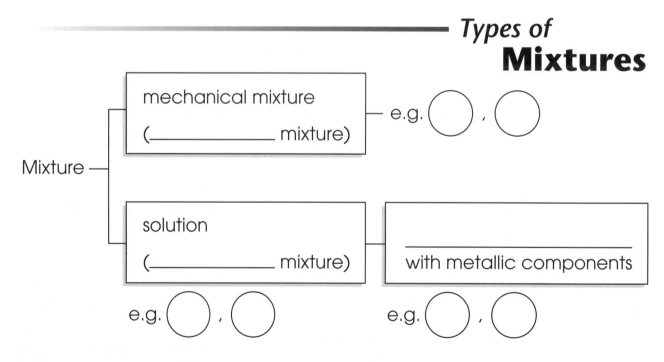

Types of **Mixtures**

Mixture

mechanical mixture

(_____ mixture)

e.g. ◯ , ◯

solution

(_____ mixture)

e.g. ◯ , ◯

_____ with metallic components

e.g. ◯ , ◯

A **brass** (copper and zinc) **keys**

B **bronze** (tin and copper) **medals**

C **sea water** (salt and water)

D **lemonade** (water and lemon juice)

E **salad dressing** (oil, vinegar, pepper)

F **concrete** (gravels, stones, sand)

C. Read the paragraphs. Then answer the questions.

Canadian coins are mixtures of different metals that cannot be mechanically separated, which means that they are solutions called alloys. Some coins are plated, or covered, with pure substances such as copper or nickel, while others are plated with alloys. For example, the loonie is plated with bronze, which is an alloy of copper and tin.

When Canadian coins were first circulated in the 1800s, they were made of metals like gold, silver, and copper. Today, coins are alloys because alloys are less expensive, more durable, and much lighter than pure metals.

Canadian Coins

94.5% steel
3.5% copper
2% nickel plating

92% steel
5.5% copper
2.5% nickel

94% steel
3.8% copper
2.2% nickel plating

91.5% nickel
8.5% bronze plating

99% nickel

92% copper
2% nickel
6% aluminum

1. Name the kind of solution that is used to make coins.

   _____

2. What is bronze made of?

   _____

3. Are coins heterogeneous or homogeneous mixtures?

   _____

4. Two metals are commonly used in the production of every coin. Sudbury, Ontario is famous for the production of one of them. Do you know what that metal is?

   _____

5. How can you make a mechanical mixture from coins?

   _____

Experiment

Introduction

Is a solution so complicated that it can only be made in a chemistry lab? Of course not! We make them, along with mechanical mixtures, every day. Do you know which ones are which though?

Take some substances you can find in and around your house and mix them with water. If they become the same throughout, they are solutions. If you can see two distinct parts, they are mechanical mixtures.

Hypothesis

Predict whether each mixture will be a "solution" or a "mechanical mixture". Write your predictions on the lines.

_____   _____   _____

Steps

1. Fill the jars half full with water.

2. Pour a tablespoon of soil into the first jar and label it "soil".

3. Repeat for salt and flour in the second and third jars.

Materials

- *3 jars*
- *1 tablespoon each of soil, salt, and flour*
- *water*
- *a spoon*
- *a pencil and paper for labelling*

4. Stir each jar well.

5. Wait 5 minutes. Then observe the jars and write your results.

Result

Label the jars and draw what you observe in each one. Write "solution" or "mechanical mixture" for each one.

Jar 1 —

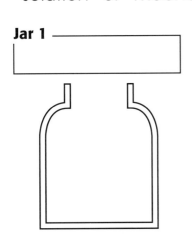

_____

Jar 2 —

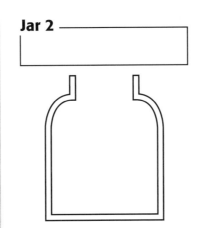

_____

Jar 3 —

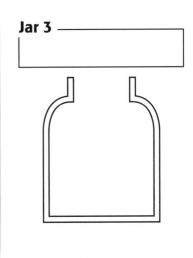

_____

Look around your house for other substances that you can test. Try mixing sugar, baking soda, or olive oil with water and record your results.

Conclusion

The hypothesis was: _____

_____

My experiment _____ the hypothesis.
              supported/did not support

4 Solutions

A solution is made up of a solute, which dissolves, and a solvent, which does the dissolving. Both can be in any of the three states of matter. We describe a solution qualitatively as "dilute" if there is less solute and "concentrated" if there is more. In this unit, you will describe solutions and identify their parts.

After completing this unit, you will

- understand that a solution is made up of a solute and a solvent, and that the solvent dissolves the solute.

- describe solutions in the qualitative terms "dilute" and "concentrated" and in quantitative terms.

> *Stir the tea until the sugar dissolves. Then it will become a tasty solution.*

vocabulary

solute: the part of the solution that is dissolved

solvent: the part of the solution that dissolves the solute

dissolve: join with another substance to make a solution

qualitative: describes the quality of a substance using words

quantitative: describes the quantity of a substance using exact measurements

sugar (solute)

water (solvent)

Have you ever noticed that when you mix certain substances with water, they become part of the liquid or "dissolve"? One example is cocoa powder. When you mix the powder with hot water, the powder dissolves into the liquid and you get hot chocolate. Look around you and make a list of the substances that dissolve in water.

Can you think of anything that does not dissolve in water?

Substances that Dissolve in Water:

cocoa powder

_____

_____

_____

_____

_____

_____

A. Fill in the blanks to complete the descriptions of solutions, solvents, and solutes. Then identify the components of the solutions and their states of matter.

made up of a 1._____ and a 2._____

Usually, the substance present in the greater amount is considered to be the solvent.

Solution

Solvent: the part of the solution that 3._____ the other part; it can be a gas, liquid, or 4._____

Solute: the part of the solution that is 5._____ ; it can be a gas, liquid, or 6._____

Sea water
(solution, liquid)
- salt
  (solute, _____)
- water
  (_____ , liquid)

Air
(_____ , _____)
- nitrogen (78%)
  (_____ , _____)
- oxygen (21%)
  (_____ , _____)

Brass
(_____ , _____)
- copper (mainly)
  (_____ , _____)
- zinc
  (_____ , _____)

B. **100 mL of grape juice is mixed with water in each jar. Write "Qualitative" or "Quantitative" for the descriptions. Then match the correct jars with the described concentrations.**

1. _____ Descriptions
   (describing concentration with words)

   ◯ most dilute

   ◯ somewhat dilute

   ◯ somewhat concentrated

   ◯ most concentrated

2. _____ Descriptions
   (describing concentration with exact measurements)

   ◯ 100 mL juice + 100 mL water

   ◯ 100 mL juice + 200 mL water

   ◯ 100 mL juice + 300 mL water

   ◯ 100 mL juice + 400 mL water

C. **Fill in the blanks.**

dissolves   qualitative   dilute
quantitative   solute

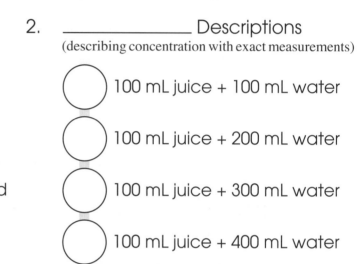

Adding solvent makes a solution more

1. _____ .

2. The terms "dilute" and "concentrated" are _____ descriptions of a solution.

3. A _____ description uses exact numbers.

4. To make a solution more concentrated, add more _____ .

5. Water is called the "universal solvent" because it _____ more solutes than any other solvent.

D. Read the paragraphs. Then answer the questions.

A substance is soluble if it can dissolve into another substance. Salt is soluble in water, but does this mean that water can dissolve an unlimited amount of salt? No, it does not! When water has dissolved all the salt it can, the resulting solution is described as saturated. Before that point, the solution is unsaturated. A saturated solution of water and salt contains 359 grams of dissolved salt for each litre of water.

Have you ever tasted sea water from the ocean? It is a solution of about 35 g of salt for every litre of water. Now, have you ever tasted the solution in a jar of pickles? It certainly contains a lot of salt. In fact, the nearly saturated salt content is exactly what deters harmful micro-organisms and preserves the pickles.

1. Is sea water a saturated solution of salt and water? If not, how much more salt is needed to make sea water saturated?

   _____

   _____

2. Describe the solution in a jar of pickles. What is its function?

   _____

   _____

3. Each container holds one litre of water. Write the least amount of salt needed to make each solution saturated. Then draw a picture of the saturated solution in the circle.

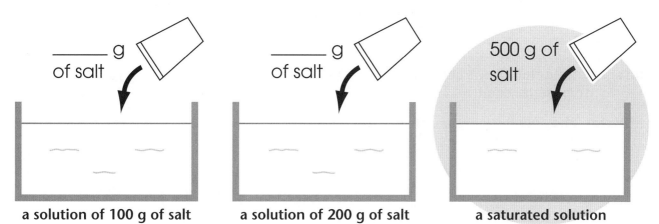

a solution of 100 g of salt   a solution of 200 g of salt   a saturated solution

5 Separating Mixtures

Just as we can join substances to make mixtures, we can separate them, too. We use different ways to separate substances, depending on the substances in the mixtures. In this unit, you will examine the different methods for separating substances in solutions and mechanical mixtures.

After completing this unit, you will

- understand that different processes are used to separate mixtures.

- understand that the process used to separate a mixture depends on the properties of its components.

Katie, you are so smart! You know how to use a sieve to separate the toys from the sand.

Vocabulary

filter: device that allows only part of a mixture to pass through

filtrate: the part of a mixture that passes through the filter

residue: the part of a mixture that remains in the filter

residue: coffee grounds

filter

filtrate: coffee

Did you know that soil is a great natural filter? Soil can separate water from a harmful mixture before it goes into a lake. This way, fish are kept safe from toxic substances. Have you ever used soap to wash your dishes on your camping trip? The soil biodegrades the soap while allowing the water to go back into the lake. Remember to use the soap at a distance from the lake or it could still contaminate the water. Did you know that you have a natural filter in your body, too? It helps filter impurities from getting into our lungs. What is it?

A. Complete what the people say with the "scientific" words.

Scientific words associated with a common separation technique	:	**filter filtrate residue**

1.

The <u>a._____</u> tastes great!
coffee

Throw the <u>b._____</u> in the grounds

compost, and <u>c._____</u> make

some more!

2.

I need some <u>a._____</u> .
air

Close the <u>b._____</u> , or screen

you'll let the <u>c._____</u> in. mosquitoes

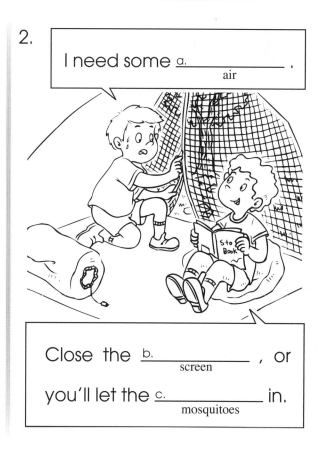

B. **Write the methods of separating mixtures, circle the correct words, and match the examples with the correct descriptions. Then answer the question.**

Methods of **Separating Mixtures**	magnetism evaporation sifting
	distillation filtration

1. _____ (e.g. ___)

   Heat a liquid mixture until one of the substances evaporates. The gas is collected into another container. It **condenses / evaporates** and becomes a liquid again.

2. _____ (e.g. ___)

   A magnet **attracts / repels** one substance in a mixture, leaving behind the substance that is not attracted to it.

3. _____ (e.g. ___)

   Heat a liquid mixture until the liquid in it evaporates into the air. That substance is gone, while the **solvent / solute** is left behind.

4. _____ (e.g. ___)

   Put a mixture of a solid and a liquid or gas into a filter. The filter collects any solid substances and allows the **liquid or gas / solid** to pass through.

5. _____ (e.g. ___)

   Put a mixture of grains of different sizes into a sieve. The sieve collects the **small / big** substances and allows the others to pass through.

6. Suggest one method that can be used to separate mechanical mixtures.

   _____

C. Read the paragraph. Then write the steps to making maple syrup and answer the question.

We often separate mixtures to extract the parts that we want from them. Do you know what separation methods are involved in making maple syrup from sap? The sap that we extract from maple trees is 97% water. We use ***evaporation*** *to reduce the water content to no more than 34%. The water is boiled away and we are left with sugary syrup. The syrup then undergoes the process of* ***filtration***, *whereby debris, such as wood bits and insects, and even some micro-organisms, such as bacteria, are removed. The syrup is then packaged in glass bottles or tin cans to be sold.*

> We don't eat the sap that comes straight from maple trees. It takes between 30 L and 45 L of sap to make 1 L of syrup.

1. **Steps to Making Maple Syrup**

A _____

B _____

C _____

D _____

2. Maple candy is more concentrated in sugar than maple syrup. How do you think you could make maple candy?

_____

_____

6 Substances and the Environment

Although both pure substances and mixtures are useful to us, they can also be harmful to the environment. In this unit, you will learn how we can dispose of substances safely and which substances we can use to reduce negative impacts on the environment.

After completing this unit, you will

- know which substances are harmful to the environment and how to dispose of them.

- know some non-toxic substances you can use as alternatives to the harmful ones.

- understand that methods of separating mixtures can be both helpful and harmful.

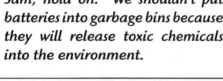

Sam, hold on. We shouldn't put batteries into garbage bins because they will release toxic chemicals into the environment.

Vocabulary

toxic/hazardous: damaging to people or the environment

biodegradable: can be decomposed by natural processes

food waste: biodegradable

Many of the cleaning products we use contain toxic mixtures that can pollute the air, land, or water. We must dispose of these products properly by taking them to our local household hazardous waste (HHW) depot. We can also make environment-friendly mixtures at home to use instead of toxic cleaning products. Below are some ideas for making environment-friendly mixtures.

Use baking soda, followed by vinegar.

Boil water and cinnamon or other spices on the stove.

A. Fill in the blanks to find out about the environment-friendly alternatives.

Environment-friendly Alternatives

1. Use alkaline, solar, or mercury-free _____ .

2. Dispose of _____ in a special landfill. Use latex paint (a non-toxic paint) instead.

3. Instead of spraying your lawn with _____ , pull weeds, spread grass seeds on the lawn, and use a lawn aerator.

4. Make your own compost to enrich the soil in your lawn instead of using _____ .

5. Dispose of toxic _____ in a HHW depot. Use non-toxic biodegradable solutions instead.

B. Complete the steps about sewage treatment using the information in the diagram.

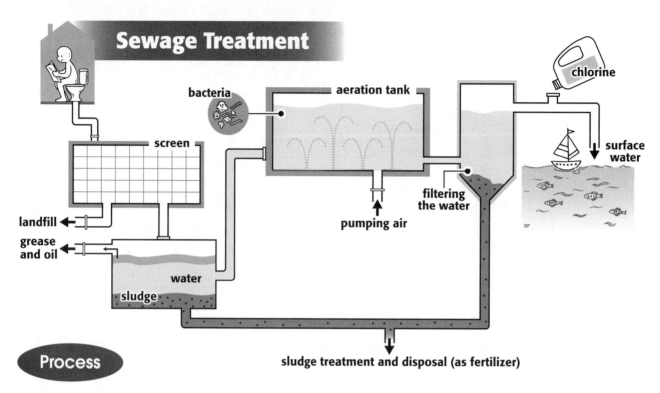

1. Remove large objects by passing the sewage through a _____ . Dump non-biodegradable materials into a _____ .

2. Scrape out the settled _____ from the water. Skim off the grease and _____ that have risen to the surface.

3. Pass water into an _____ tank. Pump _____ into the water to create an environment where _____ can feed on and digest the pollutants in the sewage.

4. _____ out the water from the remaining dirt.

5. Disinfect the water using _____ , which is later removed.

6. Discharge clean water into the _____ .

7. Properly dispose of the leftover sludge and use it as _____ if it is non-toxic.

C. Read the paragraph. Then label the diagram and answer the questions.

The crude oil that comes out of the ground must go through a refining process before we use it. We separate all sorts of fuels of different densities using distillation. Basically, crude oil is heated up. It then vaporizes and condenses. This method of separating a mixture allows us to create many products, including gasoline and plastics. However, it is extremely damaging to the environment. The refining process emits carbon dioxide and toxic chemicals, like lead, into the air. This creates smog, which is bad for our health. Refineries also produce hazardous waste that we dump onto the land, thereby polluting the environment. For these and other environmental concerns, people are looking for alternatives to oil. While we wait for scientists to come up with a solution, what can we do?

1.

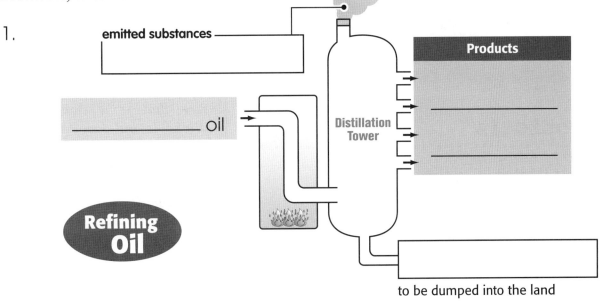

emitted substances ——————

——————————— oil

Distillation Tower

Products

Refining Oil

to be dumped into the land

2. Do you think it would be a good idea to install a carbon dioxide absorber in the emission tower? Explain.

_____

_____

3. What are the problems with the process of refining oil?

_____

_____

Experiment

Introduction

Pure water is rarely found in nature. Minerals and other substances are usually mixed in. Water that is evaporated by boiling and then condenses back into a liquid is pure. This is called distilled water.

Is the water from our kitchen tap pure? We may be pretty sure that it is clean and drinkable, but does it contain anything besides pure water? We can test it by evaporating it to see if there is anything left behind.

Hypothesis

Tap water is   pure / not pure   .

Distilled water is   pure / not pure   .

1. Clean and dry the glass jars thoroughly.

2. Pour a small amount of distilled water into one jar. Label it "distilled water".

3. Pour the same amount of tap water into the other jar. Label it "tap water".

Materials

- 2 small glass jars
- tap water
- distilled water

4. Place the jars on a sunny windowsill for as long as it takes for the water to evaporate.

5. When the water evaporates, examine the jars.

It may take a few days for all of the water to evaporate, so be patient.

Result

Draw your observation.

Distilled Water

Tap Water

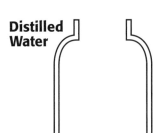

Can you think of any more water sources that you could test? Try testing different types of bottled water and rainwater to see if anything other than water is in them.

Is there any difference between what remains in the two jars? If yes, what is it?

Conclusion

The hypothesis was: _____

_____

My experiment _____ the hypothesis.
                        supported/did not support

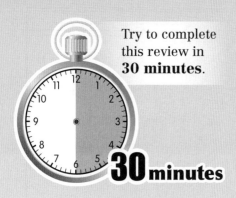

Try to complete this review in **30 minutes**.

30 minutes

This review consists of five sections, from A to E. The marks for each question are shown in parentheses. The circle at the bottom right corner is for the marks you get in each section. An overall record is on the last page of the review.

A. Write T for true and F for false.

1. Air is an example of matter. **(2)** _____

2. A dilute solution has more solute than a concentrated one. **(2)** _____

3. "Dilute" and "concentrated" are qualitative descriptions of a solution. **(2)** _____

4. An alloy is a mechanical mixture involving one or more metals. **(2)** _____

5. Water is the universal solvent because it can be dissolved into more substances than any other substance. **(2)**

_____

6. Condensation occurs when heat is taken away from a solid. **(2)**

_____

12

B. Do the matching.

1.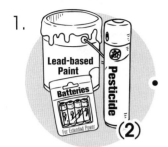

2.

3.

4.

5.

6.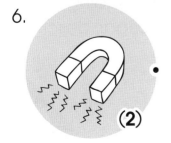

- consists of residue, a filter, and a filtrate

- substances that harm the environment

- an example of a pure substance

- a heterogeneous mixture

- an example of a solute

- attracts one substance and leaves the other substances behind

C. **Write the states of matter and draw their particles. Describe how the particles interact in each state. Then answer the questions.**

1.

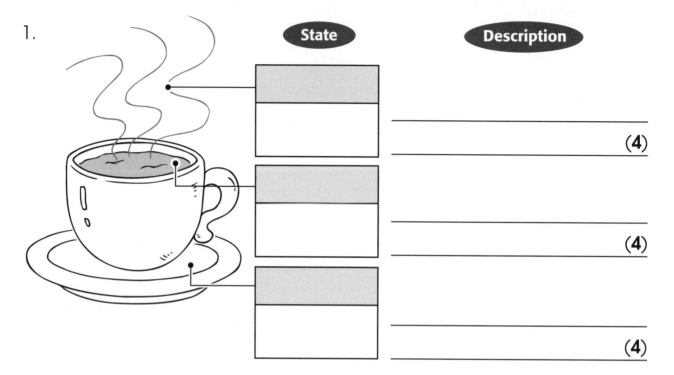

State   **Description**

_____ **(4)**

_____ **(4)**

_____ **(4)**

2. Sam puts a tea bag in a cup of hot water and takes it out after a few minutes. Is the tea a solution or a mechanical mixture? What do we call this kind of mixture? **(4)**

_____ ; _____ mixture

3. The way that we get a cup of tea from a tea bag is an example of filtration. Name the filter, filtrate, and residue. **(6)**

_____

_____

4. There are 200 mL of tea and 30 g of sugar in the cup. Is this a qualitative or quantitative description? If Sam keeps adding sugar into the cup until the tea cannot dissolve any more sugar, describe the tea qualitatively. **(4)**

a _____ description ; _____

26

D. Identify the substances in each mixture. Name and describe the methods that can be used to separate the substances. Then answer the question.

1.

A   salty water with sand

B   iron wires, sand, and gravel

substances in the mixture:

_____ **(3)**

Method 1: _____ **(2)**

_____

_____

_____ **(3)**

Method 2: _____ **(2)**

_____

_____

_____ **(3)**

substances in the mixture:

_____ **(3)**

Method 1: _____ **(2)**

_____

_____

_____ **(3)**

Method 2: _____ **(2)**

_____

_____

_____ **(3)**

2.   Define the terms "solute" and "solvent". Then name the solute and solvent in mixture A.

Solute: _____

_____ **(2)**: the solute in A: _____ **(2)**

Solvent: _____

_____ **(2)**: the solvent in A: _____ **(2)**

34

E. Check the correct answer and explain your choice.

1. The particles that have strong attractive forces: **(1)**

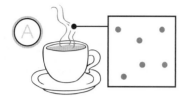  

Explain: _____

_____ **(3)**

2. From "most dilute" to "most concentrated": **(1)**

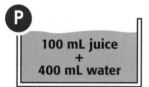 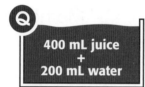 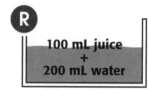 

Explain: _____

_____ **(3)**

3. The particles of a pure substance: **(1)**

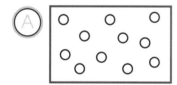 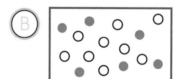 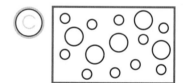

Explain: _____

_____ **(3)**

4. An environment-friendly way to get rid of weeds in your lawn: **(1)**

(A) spreading grass seeds on the lawn

(B) spraying your lawn with pesticides

(C) spraying your lawn with herbicides

Explain: _____

_____ **(3)** 16

My Record

Section **A**   12

Section **B**   12

Section **C**   26

Section **D**   34

Section **E**   16

Total

100

80-100

Great work! You really understand your science stuff! Research your favourite science topics at the library or on the Internet to find out more about the topics related to this section. Keep challenging yourself to learn more!

60-79

Good work! You understand some basic concepts, but try reading through the units again to see whether you can master the material! Go over the questions that you had trouble with to make sure you know the correct answers.

below 60

You can do much better! Try reading over the units again. Ask your parents or teachers any questions you might have. Once you feel confident that you know the material, try the review again. Science is exciting, so don't give up!

The Chemical Engineer

Arthur Fry

Chemical engineering can be interesting. We all have probably used Post-it Notes, but do you know how this invention came about? It all happened in 1970 when Spencer Silver, a chemical engineer working in the 3M research laboratories, tried to develop a strong adhesive but ended up with one that was even weaker than what he had already made. It stuck to objects, but could easily be lifted off. Silver was disappointed with this new adhesive but he did not discard it.

Then one Sunday four years later, another 3M scientist named Arthur Fry was singing in the church's choir. He used bookmarks to keep his place in the hymnal, but they kept falling out of the book. Fry remembered Silver's weak adhesive and he tried coating the bookmarks with it. The weak adhesive somehow enabled the bookmarks to stay in place and could be lifted off after use without damaging the pages. The bookmarks were an early version of Post-it Notes.

In 1980 3M made use of Silver's super-weak adhesive to make Post-it Notes. Now they have become one of the most popular office products available. Hence, in chemical engineering, a failed product can be tweaked to become a success!

Cool Science Facts

1 The Louisiana oil spill in the Gulf of Mexico in 2010 has caused huge damage to the marine environment. What did people use to clean up the oil in the sea?

2 Why are some substances such as oil and butter insoluble in water?

3 Why is a soft drink bubbly?

4 Both diamond and graphite are pure substances, and they both are made up of carbon. Why is diamond, but not graphite, the hardest material in the world?

Find the answers on the next page.

Cool Science Facts

FIGHTING OIL SPILLS

1 Instead of using chemical-based absorbents to clean up the oil in the sea, some people suggested using a natural absorbent – hair – to do the cleanup. Hair clippings were stuffed into old nylon stockings to form hair booms, which were then placed in the areas of the spill to soak up the oil. Astonishingly, each kilogram of hair is capable of absorbing as much as ten litres of oil. Since human hair is biodegradable, it is one of the safest cleaning solutions to an oil spill. Besides human hair, dog hair and feathers can also be used. If you want to learn more about how you can donate hair, fur, or nylons to help clean up oil spills, visit www.matteroftrust.org.

hair clippings

nylon stockings

2 The ability of a substance to dissolve in water is determined by whether or not the particles of this substance are attracted to the particles of water. If the particles of the substance are not much attracted to the particles of water, it is insoluble in water.

oil

water

oil

water

weak attraction force

strong attraction force

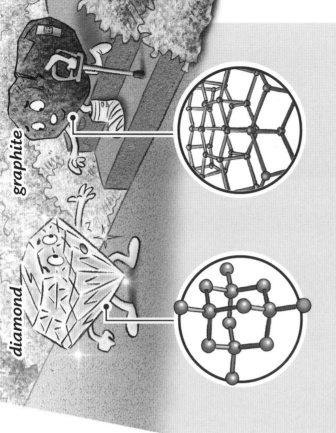

diamond

graphite

4 Diamond and graphite are made up of carbon, but the arrangements of the carbon atoms in their structures are totally different. Diamond has a cubic structure in which the carbon atoms are bonded to one another in a three-dimensional way. Graphite has a sheet-like structure in which all the atoms are only weakly bonded and lie on a plane.

3 Carbon dioxide is added to soft drinks at the end of the production process. Since the solubility of carbon dioxide increases as pressure increases, the gas is added to the liquid under high pressure until the liquid is full of the gas. When you open a can or bottle of soft drink, the pressure is released, which allows the dissolved carbon dioxide to bubble off and escape.

Understanding
Earth and Space
Systems

Scan this QR code or go to Download Centre at
www.popularbook.ca for some fun scientific
explorations!

Egg in a Bottle
Study the transfer of heat energy.

Greenhouse Effect
Investigate the effect of greenhouse gases on air
temperature.

1 Sources of Heat

Heat is a form of energy. It comes from many sources. We all need heat. We use heat to cook food and to keep us warm. In this unit, you will examine the many different sources of heat, which are either renewable or non-renewable.

heat from solar energy

heat from chemical energy

heat from mechanical energy

After completing this unit, you will

- understand that heat is a form of energy that comes from different sources.

- understand that some sources of heat are renewable and some are non-renewable.

Vocabulary

renewable: can be used again and again without running out

non-renewable: is limited and will eventually run out

fossil fuels: fuels formed from the organic remains of prehistoric plants and animals

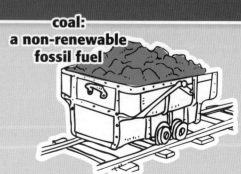

coal: a non-renewable fossil fuel

Extension

Have you ever noticed that when you are hungry, you feel colder, but once you have eaten some food, you feel much warmer? You might think that it is the result of a hot meal. Yes, a hot meal can warm you up, but even a cold meal can give you the same effect. Why? It is because your body digests the food you eat, and during this burning process, the energy stored in the food is released as heat. This heat energy warms your body. Do you know then what kind of energy is stored in food?

A. Fill in the blanks to find out the properties of heat.

Properties of Heat	space energy created transformed
	mass matter destroyed

- It does not have 1._____ , and it does not take up 2._____ .

- It is not 3._____ , but it changes matter.

- It is a form of 4._____ .

- It cannot be 5._____ or 6._____ .

heat

-  It comes from other forms of energy and can be 7._____ into other forms of energy.

B. Name the source of heat. Determine whether it is renewable or non-renewable. Then circle the correct words to complete the descriptions and answer the question.

geothermal	nuclear	electrical		biomass	food	wind
chemical	solar	mechanical		fossil fuels	hydro	

Sources of Heat

1.

   _____ energy: **renewable / non-renewable**

   This energy gives us **heat / water** and light. It is the most readily available form of natural heat energy.

2.

   _____ energy: **renewable / non-renewable**

   Heat is produced as a result of **gravity / friction**, which is caused by the mechanical forces of push and pull.

3.

   _____ energy: **renewable / non-renewable**

   This is a natural heat energy from **outside / within** the Earth. The deeper it is inside the Earth, the **hotter / better** it becomes.

4.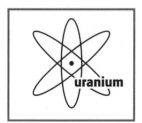

   _____ energy: **renewable / non-renewable**

   Uranium, a metal found in rocks, is used as a fuel. When uranium reacts, it releases energy to heat **water / air** to make steam-generated electricity.

5. _____ energy

This energy is generated by different forms of energy,

such as _____ energy, solar energy, and
(wind farms)

_____ energy, to produce heat.
(hydroelectric power plants)

6. _____ energy: Heat energy is released through **storing / burning** .
Below are examples of this energy.

- _____ : **renewable / non-renewable**

They are coal, natural gas, **petroleum / water** ,
etc., formed from the remains of living things that
died many years ago.

- _____ : **renewable / non-renewable**

This energy is stored in living things. It can be obtained
from **rocks / wood** , which can be burned, and
from animal waste, which produces a high-energy
gas that we can burn as the waste decays.

- _____ : **renewable / non-renewable**

Heat / Air is released during the process of digestion.

7.

Why do we shiver when we are cold?

_____

_____

_____

Shivering is a special thing our body does to maintain our body temperature. Our muscles contract and expand quickly, causing the energy stored in the muscles to be released as heat.

2 Heat and the Particle Theory of Matter

The particle theory of matter helps explain what happens to matter when it is heated. In this unit, you will revisit the particle theory of matter and learn about the effects of heat on the different states of matter.

> Let me add some ice cubes to your tea. Heat will be transferred from the tea to the ice cubes, causing the ice to melt. It will lower the temperature of your drink.

solid   liquid   gas

After completing this unit, you will

- understand how heat affects the motion of particles in solids, liquids, and gases.

- understand how the particle theory of matter explains the changes heat causes in solids, liquids, and gases.

- understand that heat can change the volume of matter.

Vocabulary

heat: a form of energy that involves the movement of particles of matter, and that is transferred from one object to another

temperature: a measurement of heat energy

volume: the amount of space a substance takes up

temperature 25°C

We measure the temperature, or the amount of heat a substance has, with thermometers. There are different types of thermometers for different purposes. For example, an infrared thermometer allows a temperature to be measured without contact – a great advantage when the substance to be measured is moving too fast, or is too dangerous, to be handled manually. Often, we need more than just to know the temperature of something; we need to control its temperature. Thermostats help us do that. Are you familiar with the instruments on the right?

fever thermometer

Check the instruments you are familiar with.

○ meat thermometer

○ weather thermometer

○ laboratory thermometer

○ fever thermometer

○ infrared thermometer

○ building thermostat

○ oven thermostat

○ fridge thermostat

A. Fill in the blanks to complete the sentences.

The Particle Theory of Matter

1.  All matter is made up of tiny _____ .
bubbles/particles

2. 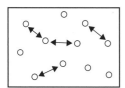 There is _____ between the particles.
air/space

3. 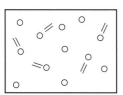 Particles are always _____ .
moving/expanding

4. 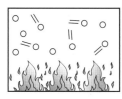 Particles move faster with increasing _____ .
heat/weight

B. **Write "solid", "liquid", or "gas" for each description. Draw to complete the particles for each state of matter in the box.**

1.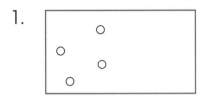

   _____

   Particles move around without any attraction to one another, allowing them to spread out and fill whatever space they are in.

2.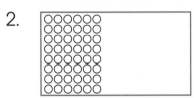

   _____

   Particles move a little, but stay in position in relation to one another.

3.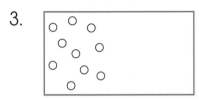

   _____

   Particles move around, staying attracted to one another, but not enough to hold a shape.

C. **Colour the picture that shows heat added in each pair. Then use the particle theory of matter to explain the changes.**

 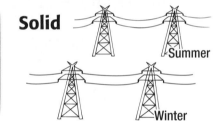

How heat affects the air inside the hot air balloon:

Gas   _____

_____

How the water changes from a liquid to a gas:

Liquid   _____

_____

Why the wires lengthen in warmer weather:

Solid   _____

_____

D. Read the paragraph. Then complete the diagram and answer the question.

You must have eaten popcorn before, but have you ever wondered why popcorn pops? Each kernel of popcorn contains a small amount of water within its strong, impervious outer covering, which is called a hull. When a kernel is heated, the water inside turns to gas. Gas particles take up more space than liquid particles do, but the gas particles are trapped by the tough hull, so pressure builds. When it comes to the point that the hull can no longer hold the pressure, the kernel explodes with a pop, allowing the gas to escape, and turning itself inside out to become the fluffy popcorn.

1. How a **Popcorn Kernel** « **Pops** »

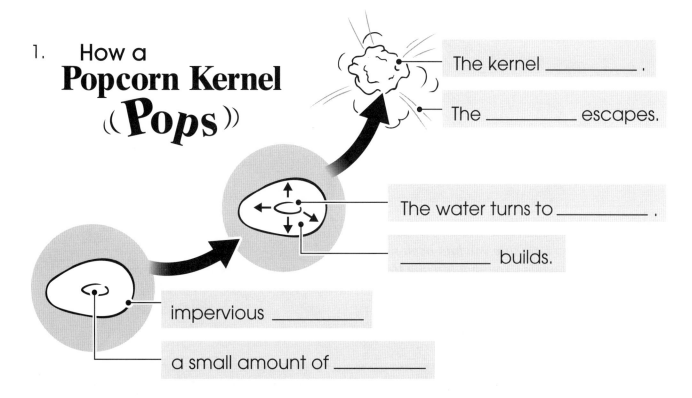

The kernel _____ .

The _____ escapes.

The water turns to _____ .

_____ builds.

impervious _____

a small amount of _____

2. Use the particle theory of matter to explain how a popcorn kernel pops.

_____

_____

_____

3 Heat Transfer: Conduction

One way that heat can be transferred from one object to another is through conduction. In this unit, you will examine the method of heat transfer through conduction. You will also learn that some materials conduct heat well, while other materials insulate people and things from heat conduction.

After completing this unit, you will

- understand that heat can be transmitted through conduction.

- understand that some materials conduct heat well, and others conduct heat poorly.

I didn't watch TV, Mom.

Heat was conducted from your body to the couch. I am sure you had been sitting here for a while. You shouldn't lie to me!

Vocabulary

conduction: the transmission of heat through matter particle by particle

thermal conductor: material that conducts heat well

thermal insulator: material that conducts heat poorly

thermal insulator

thermal conductor

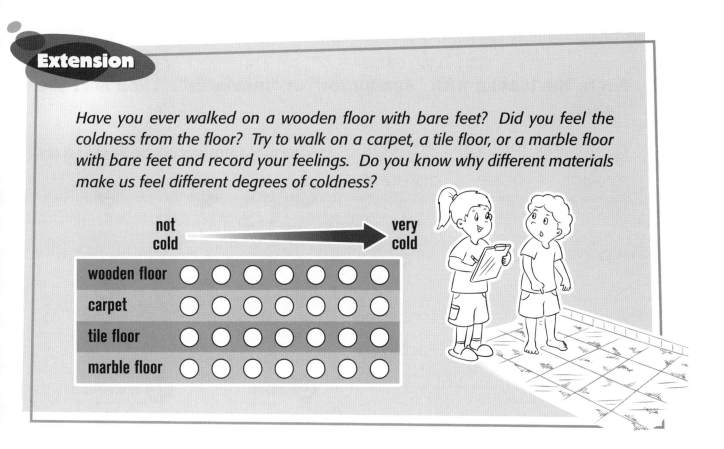

Have you ever walked on a wooden floor with bare feet? Did you feel the coldness from the floor? Try to walk on a carpet, a tile floor, or a marble floor with bare feet and record your feelings. Do you know why different materials make us feel different degrees of coldness?

A. Fill in the blanks to complete the descriptions of conduction.

Conduction in Solids	slow neighbouring
	particles vibrate faster

1.

   a metal rod

   Particles in a solid are closely packed. They _____ to and fro but they cannot change position. The vibration is _____ .

2.

   When the metal rod is heated, the particles at the hot end vibrate _____ . The fast vibrating particles bump into the slower _____ particles and make them vibrate more rapidly.

3.

   As the bumping process continues, all the _____ in the metal rod vibrate faster.

B. Fill in the blanks with "conductor" or "insulator". Then sort the items.

1. A material that lets heat pass through it easily is called a thermal _____ .

   e.g. _____

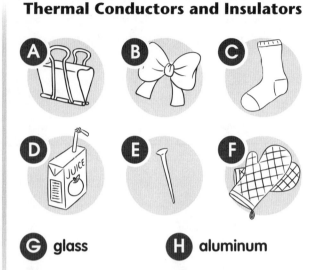

Thermal Conductors and Insulators

2. A material that does not let heat pass through it easily is called a thermal _____ .

   e.g. _____

G glass   H aluminum

I feather   J eraser

C. Show the path of heat transfer by conduction in each situation. Then circle the correct words.

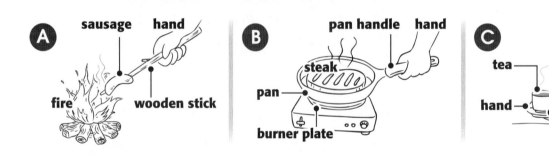

A — sausage, hand, fire, wooden stick

B — pan handle, hand, steak, pan, burner plate

C — tea, hand, cup

Heat Transfer

A   fire ⟶ _____

B   _____

C   _____

1. In conduction, heat is transferred from the **hot / cold** part to the **hot / cold** part.

2. Heat conduction between two objects occurs **with / without** physical contact between the objects.

D. Read the paragraph. Then label the diagram and answer the question.

If you have ever needed to take hot chocolate, tea, or soup from one place to another and wanted to keep it hot, chances are that you have used a vacuum flask, more commonly known as a thermos. Vacuum flasks are excellent thermal insulators. Their special design allows their hot contents to stay hot for a long time. A vacuum flask's opening is plugged with a plastic stopper. Its body consists of two thin walls of metal or glass separated by a vacuum, which is an empty space without any air. Without particles in the vacuum to allow heat to be transferred, a flask prevents conduction and is a great thermal insulator that keeps hot things, like hot chocolate, hot.

1. A Vacuum Flask

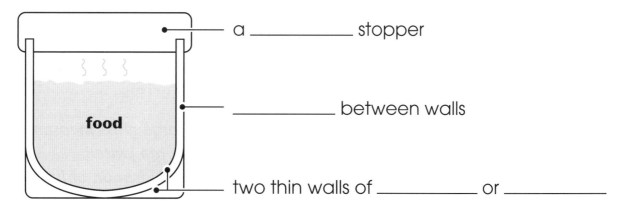

a _____ stopper

_____ between walls

food

two thin walls of _____ or _____

2. Apply the idea of conduction to explain how each part of a vacuum flask works to keep food warm.

    plastic stopper: _____

    vacuum design: _____

    _____

Experiment

Introduction

Different materials conduct heat differently. Some materials conduct heat well and some conduct heat poorly. Let's do an experiment to compare the thermal conductivity of different materials.

Guys, the drinks are hot. Watch out!

Hypothesis

Read through the experiment. Predict the thermal conductivity of the materials. Make your prediction your hypothesis.

Thermal Conductivity of Materials: _____

_____

Steps

1. Divide the butter into 4 pieces of equal size.

2. Smear a piece of butter on the outside bottom part of each cup.

Materials

- *a large glass measuring cup*
- *hot tap water*
- *a tablespoon of butter*
- *a watch with a second hand*
- *4 cups in different materials: plastic cup, ceramic cup, metal cup, glass cup*

 — **butter**

3. Fill the measuring cup with hot tap water.

4. Heat the water in the microwave oven for about 30 seconds so that it is hot but not boiling.

> *Be careful when you handle hot water. Hold the measuring cup with a cloth if needed.*

5. Pour the heated water into the cups, just above the point where the butter is on the outside.

6. Have a friend or a parent to time how long it takes for the butter to fall off each cup.

7. Record the time.

Result

Time taken for butter to fall:

_____ cup: _____ s

_____ cup: _____ s

_____ cup: _____ s

_____ cup: _____ s

Conclusion

The hypothesis was: _____

_____

My experiment _____ the hypothesis.
                    supported/did not support

4 Heat Transfer: Convection

Convection is also a form of heat transfer that takes place everywhere around us, both outside in the atmosphere and inside houses and buildings. In this unit, you will examine how and where heat transfer by convection occurs.

After completing this unit, you will

- understand that heat can be transferred through convection.
- understand the natural processes that occur due to heat transfer through convection.

Grandma, let me show you how heat is transferred by convection.

warm air

cold air

warm air

cold air

convection current

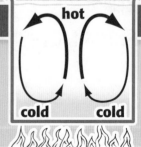

hot

cold   cold

convection: heat transfer through the movement of heated fluid

current: continuous onward movement of a body of fluid

Have you ever wondered why an entire room can be heated by an electric heater placed at one end of the room? You can try a simple experiment to see how temperature changes can create the movement of air.

Experiment: Temperature changes create a spinning spiral.

1. Cut out a circle on a piece of paper.
2. Draw a spiral line on the circle. Then cut along the line from the edge to the centre.
3. Tie a string to the centre of the spiral and hold the spiral over a warm toaster.

Watch what happens. The paper spiral starts twirling!

Can you see how the air moves?

A. Colour the arrows. Fill in the blanks to complete the descriptions.

| current | sinks | expanding | heavy | low | rises |

1. **Convection**

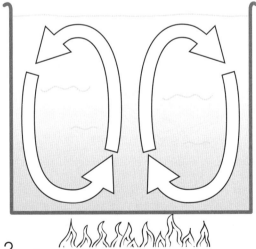

Hot Water [red ⟹]

- fast moving and _____ particles
- less dense (_____ pressure)
- _____ to the top

Cold Water [blue ⟹]

- dense and _____ particles (high pressure)
- _____ to the bottom

2. A convection _____ transfers heat from one position to another.

B. Fill in the blanks to complete the paragraph. Then check the pictures that show convection and draw the convection currents.

high	slower	liquid	particles	rises	gas	pressure	dense

Convection – a Transfer of Heat

Hot fluid – 1._____ or 2._____ – with its fast moving and expanding 3._____ , is lighter than cold fluid, which has 4._____ moving particles. Hot fluid is less 5._____ and has a low 6._____ , and cold fluid is denser and has a 7._____ pressure. Hence, hot fluid 8._____ and cold fluid falls, forming a convection current which is in a circular motion.

hot (less dense; low pressure)

hot

cold

cold (denser; high pressure)

Examples of Convection

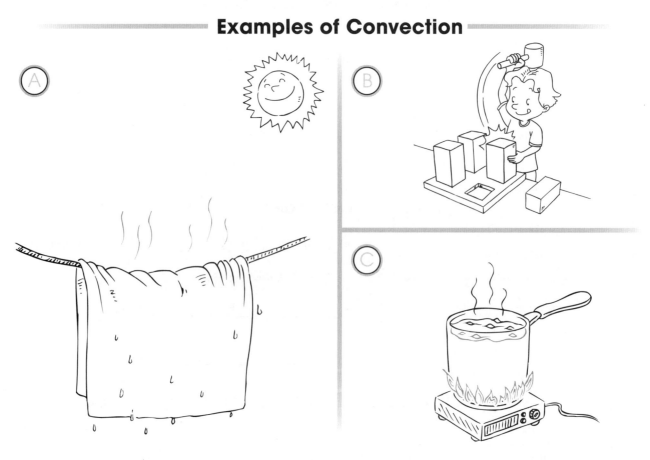

A

B

C

C. Read the paragraph. Draw the convection current and fill in the blanks to complete the diagram. Then answer the question.

*During the day, with the sun's heat, land heats up faster than water in the ocean. The air over the land gets warmer and expands. It becomes less dense and rises. The cooler, denser air over the ocean flows in as wind to take up the space previously occupied by the warm air. Since **cold** air is heavier than **hot** air, the pressure of cold air is greater. That means wind blows from areas of **high** pressure to areas of **low** pressure. It forms a convection current.*

1.

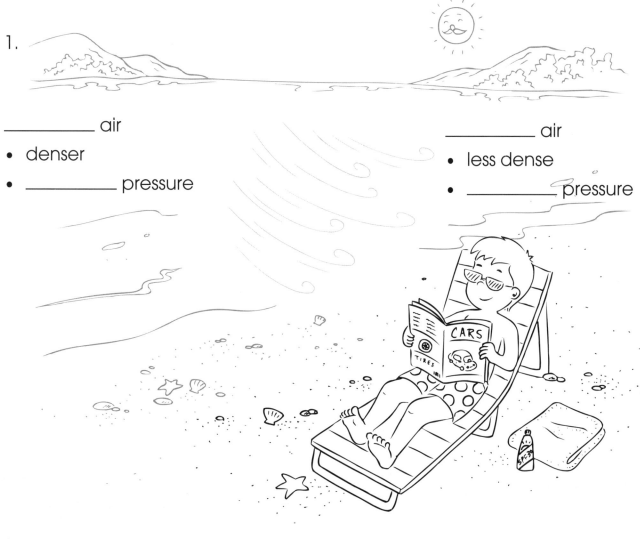

_____ air
- denser
- _____ pressure

_____ air
- less dense
- _____ pressure

2. How does wind blow during the day?

_____

_____

5 Heat Transfer: Radiation

Radiation is another form of heat transfer, by which heat travels through empty space via electromagnetic waves from the source of heat to the receiver. In this unit, you will examine the transfer of heat by radiation, and learn that some materials absorb radiated heat while others reflect it.

radiation

After completing this unit, you will

- understand that heat can be transferred through radiation.

- understand that materials can either absorb or reflect radiated heat.

Wearing something in light colours helps us stay cool in the summer because it reflects the sun's heat.

Vocabulary

radiation: heat transfer through electromagnetic waves

electromagnetic waves: rays of energy that can pass through empty space

radiation

Extension

Heat is transferred in our environment all the time. Heat from a stovetop heats the base of a kettle by conduction. Heat flows through the water in the kettle by convection.

You can also feel the heat from the stovetop even if you do not touch it. Do you know how the heat reaches you? Actually, the way that the heat from the sun travels through the vacuum of space to warm up the Earth is the same as the way that the heat from a heated stovetop reaches you. Can you come up with another example where the transfer of heat is the same as that from the sun to the Earth?

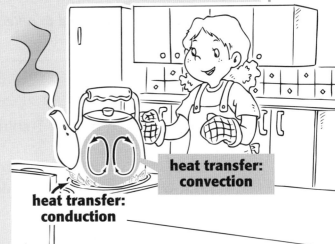

heat transfer: convection

heat transfer: conduction

A. Fill in the blanks to complete the descriptions.

| heat | conduction | radiation | vacuum | radiated |

In 1._____ and convection, objects have to touch each other in order for heat to move. 2._____ can transmit heat without direct contact between objects. The transfer of heat from the sun to the Earth through an empty 3._____ is a form of radiation. The 4._____ heat warms up the things that it meets. This explains why we can feel the 5._____ from the sun although we are not touching it.

B. Read what the girl says. Circle the correct answers. Then identify the pictures that show examples of heat transfer by radiation and explain your choice of colour.

> *Lighter materials tend to reflect radiated heat while darker materials absorb it.*

1. What would you wear to keep yourself cool on a hot day? **a dark T-shirt / a light T-shirt**

2. On a hot day, a dark T-shirt will actually have a **higher / lower** temperature because of the sun's radiation.

3. Darker materials **absorb / reflect** heat transferred by radiation.

4. Lighter materials **absorb / reflect** heat transferred by radiation.

light T-shirt   dark T-shirt

Examples of Heat Transfer by Radiation

◯ ; my choice of colour: _____
_____
_____

◯ ; my choice of colour: _____
_____
_____

◯ ; my choice of colour: _____
_____
_____

A black/white

B blue/yellow

C black/white

D dark blue/pink

E brown/green

C. Read the paragraph. Then label the diagram with the words in bold and answer the questions.

*A solar thermal collector is a device that collects the energy of the sun to heat water in a solar water heating system. A collector consists of a **metal box** with **insulation** on the sides and bottom, a coated metal **absorber plate**, and **tubes** attached to the absorber plate so that it can heat up the **cold** water flowing inside them. The heated water is then stored in a **water storage tank** for showering, laundry, and other household use. This allows you to have **hot** water available most of the time.*

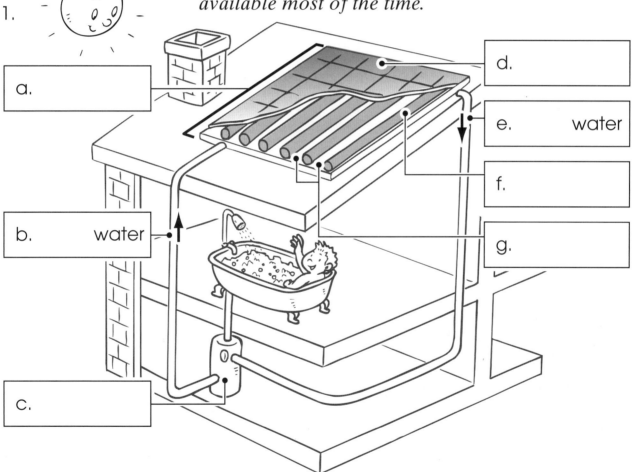

1.

a.

b. water

c.

d.

e. water

f.

g.

2. Why are the box and the absorber plate made of metal?

_____

3. What colour do you think the coating of the absorber plate is? Why?

_____

6 The Greenhouse Effect

The Earth needs the greenhouse effect to hold the warmth from the sun within its atmosphere to sustain life on Earth. In this unit, you will examine the greenhouse effect.

After completing this unit, you will

- understand the role of radiation in heating and cooling the Earth.

- understand how greenhouse gases affect the transmission of radiated heat through the atmosphere.

- know about the common sources of greenhouse gases.

Vocabulary

decomposition: breakdown or decay of organic materials

respiration: the exchange of gases in breathing

combustion: the process of burning

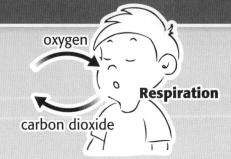

oxygen

Respiration

carbon dioxide

Extension

You probably know that a greenhouse is a structure in which plants are grown, but do you know how a greenhouse works? A greenhouse has a glass roof, letting the solar radiation in but not allowing the heat energy to escape. Hence, the temperature inside a greenhouse is higher than that outside, which makes it a favourable environment for some plants to grow. Our Earth's atmosphere works much like the glass roof of a greenhouse to maintain an average temperature of 15°C on Earth.

A. Fill in the blanks to complete the descriptions.

greenhouse　　heat　　surface　　atmosphere

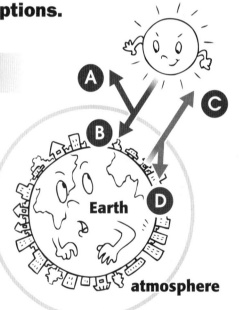

The Greenhouse Effect

A About one-third of solar radiation is reflected back to space by the Earth's _____ .

B The remaining solar radiation passes through the atmosphere and is absorbed by the Earth's _____ .

C The Earth emits its own _____ back to space.

D Some of the Earth's emitted heat is re-radiated back to the Earth by the _____ gases in the atmosphere.

B. Name the five main greenhouse gases and complete the descriptions. Then check the pictures that show sources of greenhouse gases.

water vapour   carbon dioxide   methane
ozone   nitrous oxide

fertilizers   respiration   fossil fuels

Sources of Greenhouse Gases

Main Greenhouse Gases

1. o_____
   - occurs naturally

2. w_____ _____
   - occurs naturally

3. m_____
   - from the decomposition of organic materials in wetlands
   - from the decomposition of garbage in landfills
   - from the digestive process and manure of livestock
   - from the extraction of _____

4. c_____ _____
   - from the burning of fossil fuels
   - from forest fires
   - from animal _____

5. n_____ _____
   - from fossil fuel combustion
   - from soil and nitrogen _____

C. Read the paragraph. Trace the dotted lines and fill in the blanks to complete the diagram. Then answer the questions.

Global warming refers to the rise in the average surface temperature of the Earth due to the increase in the amount of greenhouse gases in the atmosphere. These gases trap heat and prevent it from escaping from the Earth. It leads to a warmer planet and causes problems such as heavy precipitations, floods, rising water level, droughts, and wildfires. What can we do to reduce the amount of greenhouse gases released into the atmosphere?

1. **Global Warming**

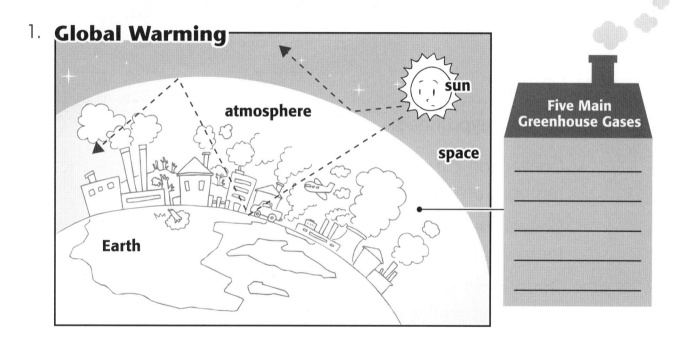

2. What problems does the increase in the amount of greenhouse gases cause?

_____

_____

3. Find books in the library or check the Internet to find two things that we can do to reduce the amount of greenhouse gases released into the atmosphere.

_____

_____

Experiment

Introduction

A difference in temperature within a fluid causes convection currents. Does it matter if there is a larger or smaller degree of difference?

hot

cold   cold

Hypothesis

Choose your hypothesis.

○ Convection currents move faster with a greater difference in temperature.

○ Convection currents move slower with a greater difference in temperature.

○ There is no change in convection currents with a greater or smaller difference in temperature.

Steps

1. Fill the food container with cold water.

2. Fill the glass with warm water.

3. Add a few drops of food colouring to the glass of water.

Materials

- *a big see-through food container*
- *a small heavy glass*
- *tap water*
- *food colouring*
- *plastic wrap*
- *an elastic band*
- *a sharpened pencil*

4. Cover the glass with plastic wrap and secure it with the elastic band.

5. Place the glass in the bottom of the food container with cold water.

6. Use the pencil to carefully poke a hole in the plastic wrap so that the coloured water starts to escape.

Do it slowly. Don't disturb the cold water.

7. Record your observations.

8. Empty the water in the food container and the glass. Repeat steps 1 to 7 with water that is colder, and then hotter, than the warm water used in the glass at the first time.

Result

Experiment 1

Temperature of water
___warm___

Description

_____
_____

Experiment 2

Temperature of water
_____

Description

_____
_____

Experiment 3

Temperature of water
_____

Description

_____
_____

Conclusion

The hypothesis was: _____

_____

My experiment _____ the hypothesis.
supported/did not support

Try to complete this review in **30 minutes**.

30minutes

This review consists of five sections, from A to E. The marks for each question are shown in parentheses. The circle at the bottom right corner is for the marks you get in each section. An overall record is on the last page of the review.

A. Write T for true and F for false.

1. Heat does not have mass, and it takes up space. **(2)**   _____

2. Friction caused by rubbing together two surfaces produces heat. **(2)**   _____

3. Heat transfer through conduction only occurs when two objects are in contact. **(2)**   _____

4. Ozone is the only gas that occurs naturally in the atmosphere. **(2)**   _____

5. Particles move faster with increasing heat. **(2)**

    _____

6. Heat is transferred from the sun to the Earth through convection. **(2)**

Earth

    _____

12

B. Do the matching.

1.
(2)

2.
(2)

- a thermal conductor

- clothing in this colour absorbs heat

3.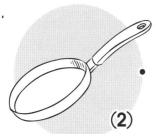
(2)

- geothermal energy – natural heat from within the Earth

- fossil fuel – a non-renewable source of heat

4.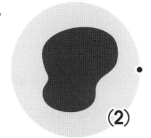
(2)

- chemical energy is released as heat during the process of digestion

5.
(2)

- uranium is a source of this energy

6.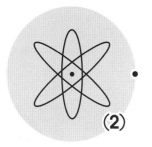
(2)

12

C. Label and draw lines to show the three forms of heat transfer in the picture. Then answer the questions.

1. **Three Forms of Heat Transfer** (9)

2. Describe the source of heat shown in the picture.

   It is a kind of **fossil fuel / biomass** . (2)

   It is a **renewable / non-renewable** energy. (2)

3. Use the particle theory of matter to explain why the wooden stick the boy is holding becomes hot. (5)

   _____

   _____

4. What would you suggest the children to wear so as to keep themselves warmer on a cold night? Explain your choice. (5)

   Choice of Clothes: **a dark blue T-shirt / a yellow T-shirt**

   _____

   _____

D. Wayne is doing an experiment to find out how heat is transferred. Look at the setting of the experiment. Then answer the questions.

1. What energy is being used to generate the light and heat energy of the lamp? **(3)**

   _____

2. Name a form of energy that can generate the energy used by the lamp. **(3)**

   _____

   I have two pieces of aluminum foil. One is painted black and one is painted white. I place them both under the lamp for two minutes.

3. Wayne touches each of the pieces of foil. What does he feel? Does he feel the same? Explain. **(5)**

   _____

   _____

   _____

4. How is the heat energy transferred from the foil to Wayne? **(5)**

   _____

   _____

5. How is the heat energy transferred from the lamp to the foil? **(5)**

   _____

   _____

E. Look at the diagram. Then answer the questions.

solar radiation

reflects

emits

absorbs

Earth

re-radiates

space

atmosphere
(contains greenhouse gases)

1. Explain how you can feel the heat from the sun. **(5)**

_____

_____

_____

_____

2. Explain the greenhouse effect with the help of the diagram. **(5)**

_____

_____

_____

3. Name two greenhouse gases and write one source for each.

_____ : _____ **(6)**

_____ : _____ **(6)**

4. The sun heats up the Earth. Use the particle theory of matter to explain how the water in the ocean changes to gas in the air. Draw the water particles in each state to support your explanation.

water in liquid form ②

_____

_____

_____

_____ **(6)**

water in gas form ②

32

My Record

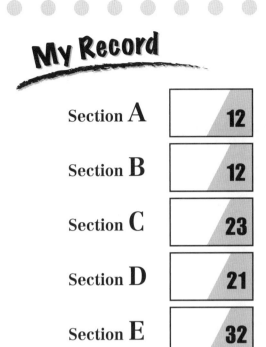

Section **A** [ ] 12

Section **B** [ ] 12

Section **C** [ ] 23

Section **D** [ ] 21

Section **E** [ ] 32

Total

100

80-100

Great work! You really understand your science stuff! Research your favourite science topics at the library or on the Internet to find out more about the topics related to this section. Keep challenging yourself to learn more!

60-79

Good work! You understand some basic concepts, but try reading through the units again to see whether you can master the material! Go over the questions that you had trouble with to make sure you know the correct answers.

below 60

You can do much better! Try reading over the units again. Ask your parents or teachers any questions you might have. Once you feel confident that you know the material, try the review again. Science is exciting, so don't give up!

The Solar Engineer

With the advance of technologies, scientists today have developed more ways to make more use of solar energy.

Solar engineers are scientists working specifically on harnessing solar energy in various ways. They use photovoltaics, for example, to convert sunlight directly into electricity. They also build concentrating solar power systems to generate heat. These systems use lenses or mirrors and tracking systems to focus a large area of sunlight into a small beam. The concentrated heat is then used as a heat source for a conventional power plant.

First Light Solar Park, located in Ontario, is the largest solar power operation built in Canada. It spans across 90 acres of land with more than 126 000 solar panels. It can generate over 10 million kilowatt hours (kWh) of renewable electricity – enough to provide power for 1000 households.

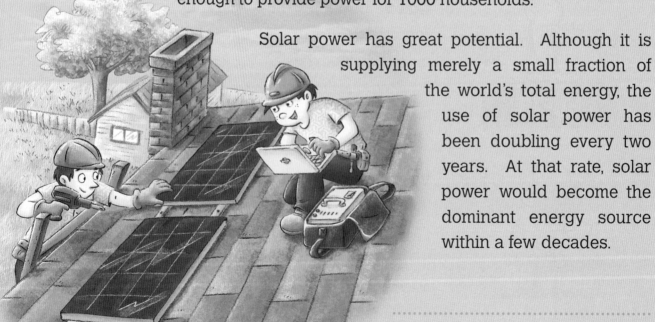

Solar power has great potential. Although it is supplying merely a small fraction of the world's total energy, the use of solar power has been doubling every two years. At that rate, solar power would become the dominant energy source within a few decades.

Cool Science Facts

1 How do self-cleaning ovens work?

2 Why do metals feel cold to the touch?

3 Why does your tongue sometimes stick to a popsicle?

4 How hot is lightning?

5 What metal has the highest melting point*?

*melting point: the temperature at which a solid becomes a liquid

Find the answers on the next page.

Cool Science Facts

1 Self-cleaning ovens use a temperature of approximately 480°C to burn off spills from baking, without the use of any chemicals. During the high-temperature cleaning cycle, the oven has a special lock system to keep the door locked, preventing us from any burn injuries. It usually takes about 3 hours to complete the cleaning process. The spills are turned into grey ash. Then all you need to do is to wipe it off with a damp sponge.

Don't get close to the oven, especially when it is in the self-cleaning mode.

Self-Cleaning

2 Metals are good conductors of heat. When you touch something metal, heat transfers away from your hand to the metal. The temperature receptors in your skin send a message to your brain that there is a drop in temperature. That is why you "feel" that the metal is cold.

heat

4

Lightning is a powerful discharge of electricity. Lightning bolts are extremely hot, with temperatures of 10 000°C to 28 000°C, which is hotter than the surface of the sun. Although the power of lightning lasts for only a few millionths of a second, things that are close to the lightning strike can get blazing hot. A lightning strike can set a tree on fire. That is why we should not stand under a tree when there is lightning.

3

When you lick a popsicle, heat transfers from your tongue to the popsicle, causing the part of the popsicle in contact with your tongue to melt. However, that part quickly refreezes together with the moisture on your tongue if the popsicle has been frozen to a very low temperature, causing your tongue to stick to the popsicle.

tungsten filament

5

The metal tungsten has the highest melting point, at 3410°C. Tungsten filaments are used in traditional light bulbs. They heat up and give out light when electric currents pass through them.

Answers

Answers

Section 1

1 Ecosystems

A. 1. ecosystem   2. living
   3. community   4. habitat
   5. organisms   6. populations
   7. rainforest ; warm ; wet ; large

B. (Individual examples)
   1. ocean ; Biotic Elements: octopus ; kelp ; dolphin ; algae ; gull
      Abiotic Elements: salt water ; rock ; sun ; sand ; air
   2. desert ; Biotic Elements: coyote ; sage ; owl ; cactus ; rattlesnake
      Abiotic Elements: rock ; sun ; sand ; fresh water ; air

C. 1. mud, water ; abiotic/abiotic
   2. Mussels, stream bed ; biotic/abiotic
   3. Young fish, insect larvae ; biotic/biotic
      insects, remains of adult fish ; biotic/biotic
   4. sediment, water ; abiotic/abiotic
      sunlight, marine plants ; biotic/abiotic

D. 1a. chlorophyll   b. photosynthesis
   c. oxygen   d. chloroplasts
   e. sugar
   2.

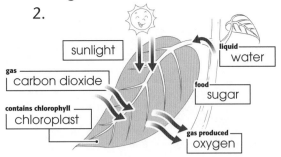

   (Colour the leaf green.)
   3. (Suggested examples)
      plants and animals ; plants and sunlight ; sunlight and carbon dioxide

2 Transfer of Energy in Ecosystems

A. 1. food   2. Herbivores
   3. Carnivores   4. fungi
   5. waste   6. nutrients
   7. growth
   8. secondary consumers
   9. primary consumers
   10. producers
   11. decomposers

B. 1.

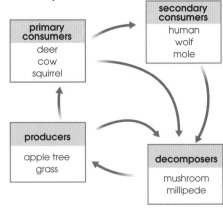

   2. They represent the transfer of energy between organisms.
   3. Yes, they can. Omnivores are primary consumers when they eat plants and secondary consumers when they eat other animals.

C. 1. organism   2. food chain
   3. eaters   4. smaller
   5. orcas   6. seals
   7. fish   8. plankton
   9. If there are too many orcas competing for food, the number of seals and fish in the area might greatly diminish.

D. 1.

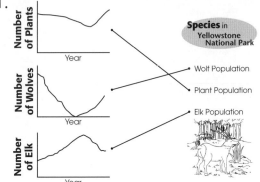

2a. wolves   b. elk   c. plants
   d. the elk population grew too high, theatening the plant life and other primary consumers in the area

3   Cycles in the Environment

A.   1. photosynthesis
    2. oxygen   3. respiration
    4. carbon dioxide

B.   1. evaporation   2. precipitation
    3. collection   4. respiration
    5. transpiration   6. condensation

C.   1. Plants   2. Bacteria
    3. animals   4. waste
    5. air

D.   1. photosynthesis
    2. respiration   3. decomposition
    4. combustion   5. ocean uptake
    6. consumption

E.   1. A: Salmon return to their birth stream to spawn.
      B: Bears fish for salmon and bring them to the shore. What they do not eat is left for other animals.
      C: Other animals eat salmon remains and then deposit them in the forest as waste.
      D: Decomposers break the salmon down into nutrients for other living things in the forest.
    2. They return to their birth stream to lay and fertilize their eggs.
    3. They die.
    4. It means the substances of which the salmon are made.

Experiment

(Individual experiment outcome)

4   Stability and Change in Ecosystems

A.   1. plants   2. slowly
    3. extinction   4. adaptations
    3 ; 1 ; 2 ; 4

B.   1. soil ; no ; growth ;
      volcanic eruption, newly exposed rock, paved areas
    2. lots of ; life ; replacement ;
      fire, hurricane, flood, agriculture, climate change, logging, landslide
    3. 2 ; 5 ; 1 ; 4 ; 3

C.   control ; increases
    1. biotic
    2. biotic
    3. abiotic
   4a. abiotic   b. abiotic
      c. abiotic   d. abiotic
    5. (Suggested answer)
      available food ; available space

D. 1a. Iceland   b. Surtsey
      1963 to 1967 ; oceanic volcanic eruptions
      Ecological succession is occurring without human interference.
    2. 1 ; 4 ; 3 ; 2
    3. B ; D ; E ; F ; I
    4. It is restricted so that succession can happen without human interference.

Answers

5 Human Activities and Ecosystems

A. Fishing: trolling ; trawler
Farming: crop rotation ; inorganic fertilizer
Logging: clear-cutting ; skidder

B. 1. introducing non-native species ; less
2. waste disposal ; polluting
3. overfishing ; less ; extinction
4. wetlands filled in for new developments ; removes
5. clear-cut logging near stream banks ; erosion
6. factory and vehicle emissions ; acid rain
7. building dams ; disrupted
8. (Suggested answer)
The land is degraded, soil is lost, and the habitat is destroyed.

C. 1. B ; C ; E ; F
(Suggested answer)
provide us with oxygen to breathe.
2. The project is called "Plant for the Planet: Billion Tree Campaign". Its goal is to encourage individuals and organizations around the world to plant one billion trees per year.
3. They suggest this so that the planted trees will grow well, produce themselves, and help boost local ecosystems instead of competing with the organisms already existing there.
4. (Suggested answers)
a. white pine   b. Western red cedar
c. acacia   d. oak

6 Controlling Human Impacts

A. 1: B   2: E   3: C
4: A   5: D   6: F

B. 1. They installed a device on the toilet that reduces the amount of water it uses.
2. They plant some native plants in their backyard.
3. They walk and ride bicycles instead of driving; they buy food from the local farmers' market to reduce pollution from transportation.

C. (Individual examples)
1. to use less of something; to use only what you need ;
turning the heat down and wearing a sweater
2. to use things more than once ;
giving clothes you have outgrown to others
3. to reprocess used materials for new things ;
returning all recyclable materials properly
4. It is in order of importance, or of what you should do first. It is most important to reduce consumption, and then to reuse things, and then to recycle them.

D. 1. forms national parks
2. manages national parks
(Suggested answers)
3. Environment Canada
4. forecasts national weather
5. studies wildlife
6-12. (Suggested answers)
6. The Ontario Ministry of Natural Resources
7. regulates what species can be hunted, and where, when, and how many can be hunted
8. regulates the activities in provincial parks
9. City of Toronto
10. regulates waste disposal
11. creates environmental programs
12. creates bylaws
13-14. (Individual answers)

Experiment

(Individual experiment outcome)

Review

A. 1. F   2. T   3. T
   4. F   5. F   6. T

B. 1.

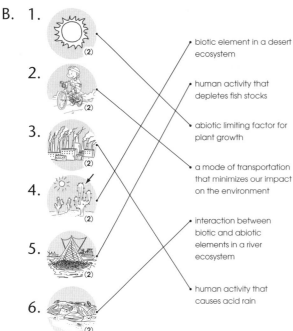

C. 1.

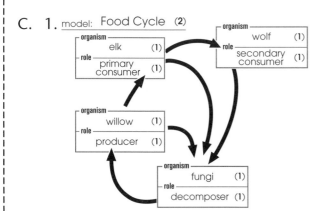

   model: Energy Pyramid
   wolf ; elk ; willow
   2a. food cycle
   b. energy pyramid

3. (Suggested answers)
 a. number of predators
 b. water supply
4. (Suggested answer)
   It might be a part of a temperate forest biome ecosystem.
5. This interaction is photosynthesis. The willow interacts with sunlight, water, and carbon dioxide to produce sugar and oxygen.
6a. The elk population would increase, which would threaten the willow population as too many elk would be consuming them.
 b. (Suggested answer)
    captive breeding program for wolves; declaring the area a national park
7a. secondary succession
 b. (Suggested answer)
    logging; an earthquake
 c. It is an example of primary succession. It is different from secondary succession in that initially, there was no soil or life on Surtsey Island like there was in the field.

D. 1. combustion
   2. atmosphere   3. photosynthesis
   4. fossil fuels   5. consumption
   6. respiration   7. ocean uptake
   8. decomposition
   9. It is essential because no new matter is produced; it is only recycled. Without recycling, matter would run out. Another example is the water cycle.

E. 1. The order is reduce, reuse, and recycle, and it is significant because it represents the order in which people should think about consumption.
   2. Shopping at a local market reduces gas emissions released by transporting food over long distances. This means the air is cleaner.

Answers

Section 2

1 Basic Structures

A. 1. A: Q   B: U
      C: R   D: T
      E: S   F: P
   2. A,Q ; B,U ; D,T ; E,S
   3. No, they do not.

B. (Individual examples)
   1. solid ; C ; G ; I
   2. frame ; D ; E ; H
   3. shell ; A ; B ; F

C. 1. shell ; frame ; hockey helmet
   2. frame ; frame ; tennis racket
   3. frame ; solid ; house
   4. frame ; shell ; tipi
   5. frame ; solid ; bridge
   6. (Individual examples)

D. 1a. a framework of connected parts,
       usually bars or beams
   b. a panel or connected panels, usually
      for the purpose of protecting or
      holding
   c. one solid piece or solid pieces piled
      together

   2a. shell   b. solid   c. shell
   d. solid   e. shell   f. frame
   g. shell   h. frame   i. shell
   j. shell/frame   k. shell   l. solid

2 Centre of Gravity

A. 1. centre   2. mass
   3. regularly   4. irregularly
   5. changes   6. stable
   7. balance

B.

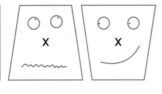

C. 1. mass ; lower to ; low

   2.    3.

   4.    5.

D. 1. Cargo ship A is more stable because
      the load is distributed evenly in the
      ship and the centre of gravity of the
      ship should be around the middle of
      the ship.
   2. The load in cargo ship A is more
      safely packed because it is evenly
      distributed so that the ship is more
      stable and less likely to flip over.

E. balance ; below

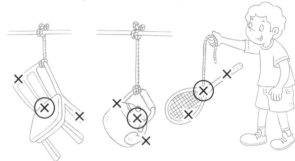

F. 1. 1 m ; 5 m ; 4.55 m
   2. The centre of gravity should be above
      the base of the building.
   3.

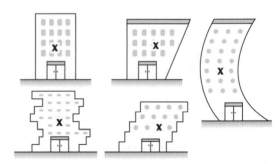

   Check: A, D

3   Forces and Structures

A. stress ;

fatigue ;

failure

(Draw a line to match each description with the corresponding picture.)

B. 1. An earthquake
    2. Still water   3. Wind
    4. Rain   5. Gravity
    6. compression   7. tension
    8. shear   9. torsion

C. 1. magnitude
    2. point of application
    3. direction
    4. direction ; B
    5. magnitude ; B
    6. point of application ; A

D. 1a. Richter Scale ; measures an earthquake's magnitude, which is obtained by recording ground movement

   b. Modified Mercalli Intensity Scale ; measures an earthquake's intensity, which is a compilation of observations regarding the earthquake's effects on structures and people

   2a. minor ; undetectable to a normal person

   great ; causing serious damage to areas several hundred kilometres away from its point of origin

   b. instrumental ; barely perceptible

   catastrophic ; total destruction

   3a. 7.0 ;

   MMI IX ; Port-au-Prince

   MMI III ; Guantanamo, Cuba

   b. (Individual answer)

Experiment

(Individual experiment outcome)

4   More about Structures

A. sameness ; two ; mirror ; B ; D

(Individual drawing)

B. 1. stability   2. base
    3. A   4. symmetrical
    5. tension   6. compression
    7. even   8. uneven
    9. C

C.

D. 1. strength   2. balanced
    3. greater

4.

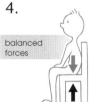

5.

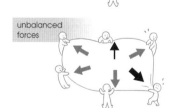

6. It is because the opposing forces are equal in magnitude when the forces are balanced.

7. If the forces are asymmetrical, the structure might break or collapse.

Answers

E. 1. A ;

1: The distance between the eyes and the screen should be 45 to 60 centimetres

2: The backrest relieves pressure from the lower back.

3: Lower arms are parallel to the floor.

4: Knees are bent at a 90° angle and thighs are parallel to the floor.

5: The chair's height from the seat to the floor is adjustable.

6: Feet must be flat on the floor or raised slightly on a footrest.

2. A ; C ; D

5 Loads and Structural Failure

A. 1. force   2. load
   3. Gravity   4. roof
   5. snow   6. wind
   7. greater   8. collapse
   9. failure

B. 1. poor design ; high
   2. unsuitable materials ; rusting
   3. oversized loads ; snow
   4. foundation failure ; sinking
   5. poor workmanship ; poorly

C. 1. bigger ; lower
   2. Put a coating over the existing iron to slow down and prevent rusting or replace it with materials that do not rust.
   3. The roof should be more slanted so that snow can slide off it to minimize accumulation.
   4. The building should be built on a sturdy and level ground.
   5. Replace the poorly crafted beams with some that fit the frame.

D. 1. Remove the top deck and make the vehicle wider or longer instead.
   2. Use sturdy materials, such as wood instead of cardboard and nails instead of staples.

E. 1.

2. The bridge was built to be slender and very long, but the relatively thin steel girders were not strong enough to support the deck.

3. The force of wind triggered the collapse of the bridge. The torsion force was in action before the bridge fell.

4. B

6 Materials and Structures

A. A: Cloth ; torsion
   B: Felt ; shear
   C: Rope ; tension
   D: Wood ; compression

B. (Suggested answers)
   1. warmth ; water resistance ;
      cotton ; vinyl ;
      Cotton keeps one's feet warm and vinyl prevents water from seeping into the boots.
   2. weight ; durability ;
      aluminum ; plastic ;
      Aluminum and plastic are both durable and lightweight for travelling.

3. strength ; transparency ;
   plastic ; aluminum
   Plastic wrap allows the covered food
   to be seen clearly and the aluminum
   serrated edge makes it easy to tear a
   piece of wrapping.
4. weight ; durability ;
   steel ; concrete ;
   Steel is durable and concrete is heavy
   enough to withstand natural forces,
   like strong winds.

C. 1. cost   2. availability
   3. aesthetic   4. aesthetic
   5. no
   6. (Individual answer)

D. 1. (Individual colouring)
   (Suggested answers)
   strong ; durable ; lightweight
   2. Plastic bags that end up in landfills
      take hundreds of years to break
      down. They suffocate wildlife, pollute
      water, and release toxic materials into
      the environment.
   3. reusable shopping bag ;
      A ; C ; E ; G ; H ; I ;
      The material will still be durable after
      being reused many times. It can also
      be broken down in a short period of
      time when disposed of.

Experiment

(Individual experiment outcome)

Review

A. 1. T   2. F   3. F
   4. T   5. T   6. F

B. 1.

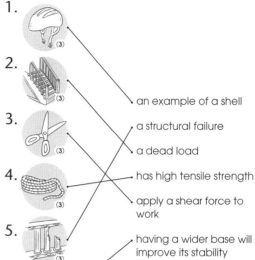

C. 1. frame ; a framework of connected
      parts
      shell ; used for the purpose of holding
   2. C ; The heavier base lowers the centre
      of gravity, making the pencil holder
      more stable.
   3. No, it will not because plastic wrap is
      too flexible to be a shell.

D. 1.

Can support...

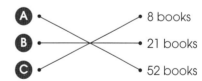

A → 52 books
B → 8 books
C → 21 books

The materials used in stool A are
sturdier than those in stool C; hence,
it is able to support a heavier load.
Stool A also has a symmetrical design,
so it is more stable than stool B.

2. He should make the legs of the stool
shorter so that the centre of gravity
is lowered, making the stool more
stable.

3. the variable weight of forces acting on a structure ;

the weight of forces that are part of a structure ;

live ; dead

E. 1. A ; B ; The top of the diving board must have tensile strength and the bottom of it needs compresssive strength.

2. C ; The arrows have the same size and are pointing in the correct directions.

3. B ; The amount of force on an object depends on direction. Wagon B has the greatest force acting on it to move it to the left.

4. A ; Brick is a sturdier and heavier foundation than sponge, and structure A is symmetrical.

Section 3

1 The Particle Theory of Matter

A. 1. particles   2. moving

3. space   4. Heat

5. the same   6. forces ; weak

B. 1. ; solid ; close ; barely ; bottle ; (Individual example)

2. ; liquid ; space ; slip ; water ; (Individual example)

3. ; gas ; most ; directions ; helium ; (Individual example)

C. 1.

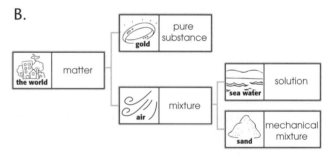

2. smallest   3. gases

2 Pure Substances and Mixtures

A. 1. mixture ; mixture ; pure substance

2. pure substance ; pure substance ; mixture

3. pure substance ; pure substance ; mixture

B.

C.

D. 1. pure ;

lustre: high ; malleability: high ; conductivity: high ; reactivity: no

2a. copper ; used in roofing and can be corroded, meaning that it reacts with air to develop a green coating

b. iron ; used to build ships and cars, and rusts when it reacts with air and water

c. (Individual answer)

3 Solutions and Mechanical Mixtures

A. 1. mechanical mixture
2. properties
3. different
4. heterogeneous
B ; C

B. 1. homogeneous
2. solution   3. metal
4. alloy   5. heat

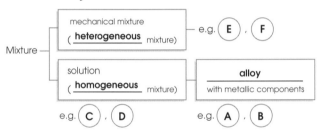

C. 1. alloy   2. copper and tin
3. homogeneous
4. nickel
5. Put them together into a collection.

Experiment

(Suggested experiement result)
Result: soil – mechanical mixture ;
salt – solution ;
flour – mechanical mixture

4 Solutions

A. 1. solute   2. solvent
3. dissolves   4. solid
5. dissolved   6. solid

Sea water: solid ; solvent
Air: solution ; gas
solvent ; gas
solute ; gas
Brass: solution ; solid
solvent ; solid
solute ; solid

B. 1. Qualitative ; B ; D ; C ; A
2. Quantitative ; A ; C ; D ; B
C. 1. dilute   2. qualitative
3. quantitative   4. solute
5. dissolves
D. 1. Sea water is not a saturated solution. 324 more grams of salt are needed to make one litre of sea water saturated.
2. It is a nearly saturated solution of salt and water. It preserves the pickles by deterring harmful micro-organisms.
3a. 259   b. 159
c.

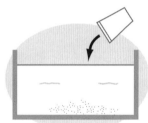

a saturated solution

5 Separating Mixtures

A. 1a. filtrate   b. residue
c. filter
2a. filtrate   b. filter
c. residue
B. 1. distillation ; B ; condenses
2. magnetism ; D ; attracts
3. evaporation ; A ; solute
4. filtration ; C ; liquid or gas
5. sifting ; E ; big
6. (Any one of the following)
sifting ; filtration ; magnetism

Answers

C. 1. A: Extract sap from a maple tree.
   B: Evaporate excess water.
   C: Filter out debris and micro-organisms.
   D: The syrup is packaged.
2. Evaporate more of the water contained in the sap.

6 Substances and the Environment

A. 1. batteries   2. lead-based paint
   3. pesticides   4. chemical fertilizers
   5. cleaning products
B. 1. screen ; landfill
   2. sludge ; oil
   3. aeration ; air ; bacteria
   4. Filter
   5. chlorine
   6. surface water
   7. fertilizer
C. 1.

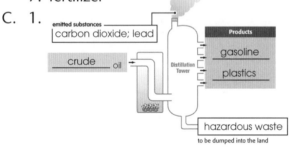

2. Yes, it would be a good idea because it would reduce carbon dioxide emissions.
3. The refining process emits toxic chemicals into the air and produces hazardous waste that pollutes the land.

Experiment

(Suggested result)
Result: Yes. Some particles remain in the tap water jar, but not in the distilled water jar.

Review

A. 1. T   2. F   3. T
   4. F   5. F   6. F

B. 1.

2.

3.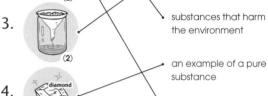

4.

5.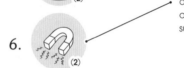

6.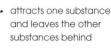

- consists of residue, a filter, and a filtrate
- substances that harm the environment
- an example of a pure substance
- a heterogeneous mixture
- an example of a solute
- attracts one substance and leaves the other substances behind

C. 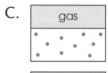 Particles spread apart and move in all directions.

 Particles move and slip past each other.

 Particles are packed tightly together and can barely move.

2. solution ; homogeneous
3. The filter is the tea bag, the filtrate is the tea, and the residue is the tea leaves.
4. quantitative ; saturated

D. 1. **Mixture A**: salt, sand, water

Method 1: filtration

By passing the mixture through a filter, the sand is removed (residue) from the salty water (filtrate).

Method 2: distillation

By distilling the salty water, the water is removed from the salt, which is left behind. The water evaporates and then condenses into another container.

Mixture B: iron wires, sand, gravel

Method 1: sifting

By passing the mixture through a sieve, the sand will fall through and the iron wires and gravel will be collected in the sieve.

Method 2: magnetism

A magnet will attract the iron wires and leave the gravel behind.

2. the part of a solution that dissolves into the solvent ; salt

the part of a solution that dissolves the solute ; water

E. 1. C ; Particles in solids have strong attractive forces to keep them tightly packed together.

2. C ; Water is the solvent and juice is the solute. The more concentrated solutions have more juice in proportion to the amount of water they contain.

3. A ; All of the particles in a pure substance are the same.

4. A ; Spreading grass seeds can maintain a healthy lawn without the use of toxic chemicals.

1   Sources of Heat

A. 1. mass   2. space
   3. matter   4. energy
   5. created   6. destroyed
   7. transformed

B. 1. solar ; renewable ; heat
   2. mechanical ; renewable ; friction
   3. geothermal ; renewable ; within ; hotter
   4. nuclear ; non-renewable ; water
   5. electrical ; wind ; hydro
   6. chemical ; burning
      fossil fuels ; non-renewable ; petroleum
      biomass ; renewable ; wood
      food ; renewable ; Heat
   7. Our body tries to release energy stored in our muscles as heat to maintain our body temperature.

2   Heat and the Particle Theory of Matter

A. 1. particles   2. space
   3. moving   4. heat

B. 1.   ; gas

   2. ; solid

   3. ; liquid

C.

Gas: The particles move faster, bumping one another out, so the air becomes less dense than the air outside.

Liquid: As the particles move faster with increased heat, they start to escape as gas.

Solid: The particles in the power lines move faster and expand when they get warm, so they sag a bit more.

D. 1.

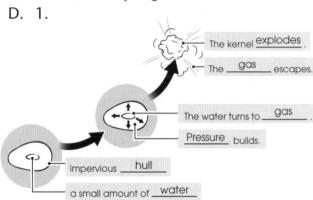

The kernel __explodes__ .

The __gas__ escapes.

The water turns to __gas__ ,

__Pressure__ builds.

impervious __hull__

a small amount of __water__

2. When heated, the water particles inside a kernel move faster and the water turns to gas. The gas particles move even faster, and pressure builds within the strong hull until the kernel explodes, allowing the fast moving air particles to escape.

3 Heat Transfer: Conduction

A. 1. vibrate ; slow
   2. faster ; neighbouring
   3. particles

B. 1. conductor ; A, E, H
   2. insulator ; B, C, D, F, G, I, J

C. A: fire → sausage → wooden stick → hand
   B: burner plate → pan → steak and pan handle → hand
   C: tea → cup → hand
   1. hot ; cold
   2. with

D. 1. plastic ; vacuum ; metal ; glass
   2. plastic stopper:
      Plastic is a thermal insulator, so it can prevent heat loss through conduction.
      vacuum design:
      A vacuum contains no particles to allow the transfer of heat, so it makes a great thermal insulator to prevent heat loss through conduction.

Experiment
(Individual experiment outcome)

4 Heat Transfer: Convection

A. 1.

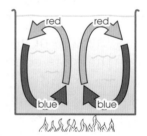

Hot Water: expanding ; low ; rises
Cold Water: heavy ; sinks
   2. current

B. 1. liquid   2. gas
   3. particles   4. slower
   5. dense   6. pressure
   7. high   8. rises

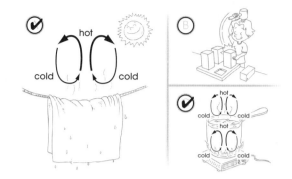

C. 1.

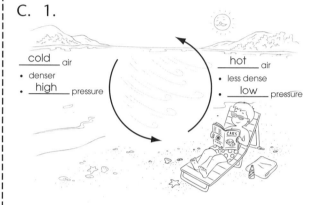

2. Wind blows from the ocean, where air is cooler and denser, to the land, where air is warmer, lighter, and less dense.

5 Heat Transfer: Radiation

A. 1. conduction   2. Radiation
   3. vacuum   4. radiated
   5. heat

B. 1. a light T-shirt 2. higher
   3. absorb   4. reflect

A ; white ;

A white beach umbrella reflects heat and keeps you cool under the sun.

C ; white ;

A white cooler reflects heat and keeps the food or drinks inside it cold for a longer period of time.

D ; dark blue ;

A dark blue coat absorbs heat and makes you warm in cold temperatures.

C. 1a. metal box
    b. cold
    c. water storage tank
    d. absorber plate
    e. hot
    f. tubes
    g. insulation

2. It is because metal is a good conductor of heat.

3. It is black because dark colours absorb heat.

6 The Greenhouse Effect

A. A: atmosphere
   B: surface
   C: heat
   D: greenhouse

B. 1. ozone
   2. water vapour
   3. methane ; fossil fuels
   4. carbon dioxide ; respiration
   5. nitrous oxide ; fertilizers
   A ; C ; D

C. 1. (Trace the dotted lines.)
     ozone ; methane ; water vapour ; carbon dioxide ; nitrous oxide

2. It causes heavy precipitations, floods, rising water level, droughts, and wildfires.

3. (Individual answer)

Experiment
(Individual experiment outcome)

Review

A. 1. F   2. T   3. T
   4. F   5. T   6. F

B. 1.

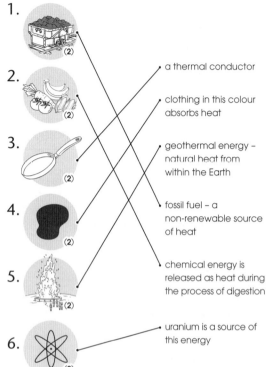

C. 1.

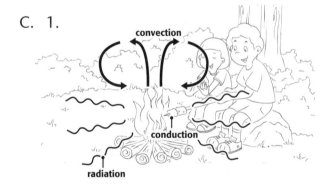

2. biomass ; renewable
3. With heat from the fire, particles in the wooden stick move faster, bumping one another and transferring heat to the entire stick.
4. I would suggest that they wear dark blue T-shirts because dark colours absorb heat.

D. 1. electrical energy
2. (Suggested answer)
   hydro energy
3. He will feel that the two pieces of foil are hot, but the black one will be hotter than the white one because dark colours absorb heat whereas light colours reflect it.
4. The heat energy is transferred from the foil to Wayne through conduction.
5. The heat energy is transferred from the lamp to the foil through radiation.

E. 1. I can feel the heat from the sun because heat is transferred from the sun through empty space via electromagnetic waves to reach the Earth by radiation.
2. The Earth absorbs the heat from solar radiation and emits its own heat back to space, but some of the heat is re-radiated back to the Earth by the greenhouse gases in the atmosphere, and this warms up the Earth.
3. (Suggested answer)
   carbon dioxide ; from animal respiration
   nitrous oxide ; from soil and nitrogen fertilizers
4.

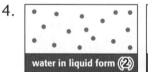
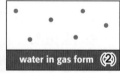

Particles of the liquid water in the ocean move around, staying attracted to one another. With the sun's heat, the particles move faster, bumping one another out, and escape as gas.

TRIVIA

Questions

David Bushnell invented the first submarine in 1775. What did he call his submarine?

A. Bushnell
B. Nutshell
C. Acorn
D. Turtle

Is the Earth's crust thinner under oceans or under mountains?

True or False

All mammals drink water.

What is a blue moon?

A. a moon that is blue in colour
B. the second full moon in a month
C. one of the moons of Mercury

Answer:

D. Turtle

He called it the Turtle because that was what it looked like underwater.

Answer:

under oceans

Generally, the higher a mountain, the thicker the Earth's crust under it is.

Answer:

false

Marine mammals, such as whales and dolphins, do not drink sea water because it is too salty. They get their water from the food they eat instead.

Answer:

B. the second full moon in a month

In every century, there are just 41 months with two full moons.

True or False

Plastic bottles do not decompose in the ground.

Deserts are very dry places, so it is impossible to see a rainbow in a desert.

Why are coral reefs called the "rainforests of the sea"?

A. They receive a lot of rain.

B. There is a lot of oxygen there.

C. They contain many different kinds of species.

The Toronto City Hall is nicknamed "The Eye of Government". How did it get this nickname?

A. The bird's-eye view of the building looks like an eye.

B. The building is located in the heart of Toronto.

C. The building is secured with over 200 surveillance cameras.

Answer:

false

Plastic bottles do decompose, but it takes at least several hundred years for them to decompose.

Answer:

false

There are still times when it rains in deserts. With sunlight and raindrops in the air, rainbows can form.

Answer:

C. They contain many different kinds of species.

Although coral reefs cover less than 1% of the world's oceans, they are home to 25% of all species of marine life.

Answer:

A. The bird's-eye view of the building looks like an eye.

When you look down at the council high up from the air, the council chamber located between the towers looks like the pupil of an eye, whereas the two towers look like the upper and lower eyelids.

Does sound travel faster in warm air or cold air?

What was the coldest recorded temperature on Earth?

A. -89.2°C

B. -121.7°C

C. -250°C

True or False

"Centi" means hundred and "peds" means feet, so centipedes have 100 feet.

How much water is used in a five-minute shower?

A. about 3 litres

B. about 30 litres

C. about 300 litres

Answer:

warm air

Sound travels faster in warm air because the particles in warm air move faster than those in cold air.

Answer:

A. -89.2°C

It was recorded in Vostok, Antarctica on July 21, 1983.

Answer:

false

Centipedes have anywhere from 20 to 300 feet.

Answer:

B. about 30 litres

With a low-flow shower head, about 30 litres of water are used. With a high-flow shower head, 75 litres or even more are used.

Camels can survive for a long time without drinking because their humps store a large amount of water.

True or False

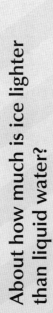

All planets but one in our solar system rotate counter-clockwise. Which planet rotates clockwise?

About how much is ice lighter than liquid water?

A. 1%   B. 9%

C. 20%   D. 50%

Aside from melting the polar ice caps, global warming causes some species to...

A. produce more offspring.

B. drink more water.

C. swim more.

Answer:

false

Camels store water in their bloodstreams. Their humps store fat.

Answer:

Venus

Venus is the only planet in our solar system that rotates clockwise.

Answer:

B. 9%

This is why ice always floats.

Answer:

A. produce more offspring.

Since it gets warmer earlier in the spring, some species such as butterflies and moths have a longer period of time to find mates.

Moai are massive human figures with very large heads that are carved from rocks. Out of all moai discovered, only one of them has legs. What is the posture of that moai?

A. kneeling   B. running

C. dancing   D. jumping

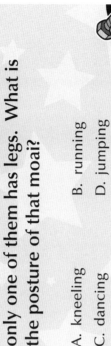

Canada is home to the oldest rocks found on Earth. Where were these rocks found?

A. along the northern Quebec coast of Hudson Bay

B. in the Rocky Mountains in northern British Columbia

C. along the southern Ontario coast of Lake Ontario

Why do polar bears not eat emperor penguins?

A. Emperor penguins' distinctive smell scares off polar bears.

B. Polar bears prefer eating seals.

C. Polar bears cannot find emperor penguins because they live too far apart.

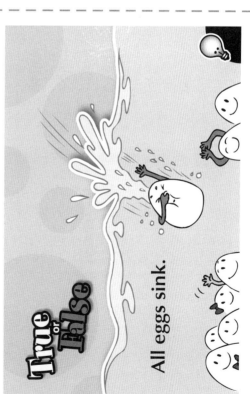

True or False

All eggs sink.

Answer:

A. kneeling

This kneeling moai is called Tukuturi.

Answer:

C. Polar bears cannot find emperor penguins because they live too far apart.

Polar bears live in the Arctic while emperor penguins live in the Antarctic.

Answer:

A. along the northern Quebec coast of Hudson Bay

These rocks were found in 2008 and are estimated to be 4.28 billion years old.

Answer:

false

Fresh uncooked eggs always sink, but cooked eggs and rotten eggs always float.

The Leaning Tower of Pisa leaned to the southeast when it was first built. However, the loose soil has made the tower shift direction. Which direction does the tower now lean to?

What colour is the metal mercury?

A. light blue
B. silvery-white
C. colourless

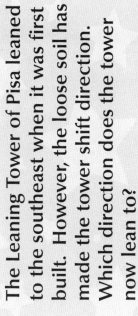

True or False

Humans are the largest group of organisms on Earth.

True or False

Like the sun, you can see the North Star no matter where you are.

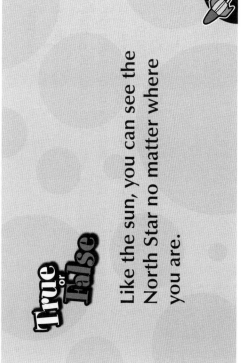

Answer:

southwest

Answer:

B. silvery-white

Answer:

false

Insects are the largest group of organisms; they make up 95% of all animal species on Earth.

Answer:

false

One can only see the North Star in the northern hemisphere. It is impossible to see the North Star in countries in the southern hemisphere, such as Australia.

What are eyelashes for?

A. opening up the eyes
B. keeping the eyes warm
C. preventing debris from getting into the eyes

True or False

At rest, moths usually spread their wings out to their sides, whereas butterflies fold their wings above their backs.

True or False

The human body emits radiation.

Which two countries emit the most carbon dioxide?

Answer:

C. preventing debris from getting into the eyes

Answer:

true

Answer:

true

The human body emits radiation as a result of heat energy to keep warm and provide power for every part of the body.

Answer:

China and the U.S.

They emit about 40% of the carbon dioxide emitted in the world.

Which planet would float on water if there were a container big enough to place the planet in?

A. Venus   B. Earth

C. Jupiter   D. Saturn

Can rabbits vomit like humans do?

Which one is the largest and heaviest cat in the cat family?

A. tiger

B. lion

C. leopard

True or False

Water absorbs light.

Answer:

D. Saturn

Saturn is the only planet that is less dense than water.

Answer:

A. tiger

Answer:

No, they cannot.

The esophagus of a rabbit can only move things in one direction, which is towards its stomach.

Answer:

true

This is why the bottom of an ocean is always in complete darkness, as 99% of sunlight has already been absorbed at a depth of 150 m.

Which instrument was first made in China out of bones in 500 BCE?

A. flute

B. drum

C. triangle

D. shaker

True or False

Ocean currents flow clockwise in both northern and southern hemispheres.

Which involuntary activity are astronauts unable to do in space?

A. sneeze   B. burp

C. blink   D. shiver

True or False

You are shorter at the end of the day than you are in the morning.

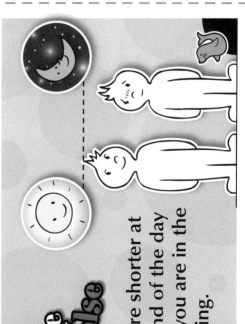

Answer:

A. flute

Answer:

false

Ocean currents flow clockwise in the northern hemisphere and counter-clockwise in the southern hemisphere.

Answer:

B. burp

We need gravity to burp. There is no gravity in space to separate liquid from gas in the astronauts' stomachs, so they cannot burp.

Answer:

true

The spine compresses throughout the day due to gravity, but expands again when you are sleeping.

How long does it take moonlight to reach the Earth?

A. 1.25 seconds

B. 1.25 hours

C. 1.25 days

True or False

Since there are many more species living in rainforests than in deserts, it must be true that rainforests occupy more land than deserts.

What was used to brush teeth in 3000 BCE?

A. scattered eggshell

B. a twig with a frayed end

C. finely grained salt

D. leaves with rough surfaces

True or False

If the highest mountain could be put in the deepest part of the ocean, we could still see its peak.

Answer:

A. 1.25 seconds

Answer:

B. a twig with a frayed end

It was also called a "chew stick".

Answer:

false

Rainforests and deserts take up about 6% and 30% of the Earth's land surface respectively.

Answer:

false

Mount Everest, the highest mountain, is 8848 m above sea level, whereas the Challenger Deep, the deepest point in the ocean, is almost 11 000 m below sea level.

True or False

Earthworms cannot tell day and night because they have no eyes.

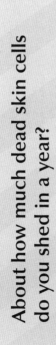

Which one is the most abundant element in the universe?

A. hydrogen

B. oxygen

C. iron

About how much dead skin cells do you shed in a year?

A. about 500 g   B. about 1 kg

C. about 4 kg   D. about 10 kg

True or False

The Great Barrier Reef is the only natural structure that you can see from space.

Answer:

false

Earthworms do not have eyes but their skin can detect light.

Answer:

A. hydrogen

Stars are mainly composed of hydrogen, and stars are the most abundant bodies in the universe. Hydrogen makes up about 75% of all matter.

Answer:

C. about 4 kg

New skin cells are always forming and it takes them 2 to 4 weeks to move from the bottom to the surface of the epidermis, the top layer of your skin.

Answer:

true

The Great Barrier Reef stretches over 2600 km, covering an area of about 344 400 km^2.

True or False

Using laptop computers instead of desktop computers save energy.

Which of the following does not belong?

A. sickle   B. chisel

C. hammer   D. knife

In order to swim out of water, how many times does a flying fish need to move its tail in one second?

A. 2 times   B. 10 times

C. 70 times   D. 400 times

Our Earth has one moon. How many moons does Mars have?

A. 1   B. 2

C. 10   D. 16

Answer:

true

Laptop computers can use up to 80% less energy than desktop computers.

Answer:

C. hammer

The others are cutting tools.

Answer:

C. 70 times

A flying fish needs enough speed to leap out of water.

Answer:

B. 2